Paul Robert. was born in 1953 and grew up in a caravan in Oxford. His father was a radical Marxist and his mother the daughter of Russian-Romanian Jewish immigrants. His lifelong passion for the violin began when he was eight years old, and he went on to lead the Medici String Quartet, of which he was a founder member. He explored the connection between healing and music in the Channel 4 series *Music and the Mind*, and formed unique collaborations with the pianist Sir Clifford Curzon, Sir John Tavener and the Royal Shakespeare Company amongst others. He was recognised with numerous honorary degrees and was a fellow of the Royal Society of Arts and the National Endowment for Science, Technology and the Arts. He died in July 2016.

Further praise for *Soundscapes*:

'Like Dusinberre he focuses on Beethoven, but this is also an extremely personal book, in which a near-death experience as the result of a stroke leads to an idiosyncratic but absorbing meditation on the relationship between music and mysticism.' Adam Lively, *Sunday Times*

'In 2008, during an operation to repair a torn aorta, Robertson spent a lengthy period clinically dead. From his out-of-body experiences grows a new understanding. The leader of the Medici String Quartet . . . tells of becoming a musician, his mentors, his life with the string quartet, and how music can aspire to a higher state of consciousness.' Richard Fairman, *Financial Times*

'A delightful memoir full of bizarre anecdotes, intriguing thoughts and, most of all, amusing stories . . . An extraordinary man's life and its deep links to the music that has always been his guide . . . An engaging, guileless book.' *Jewish Chronicle*

Soundscapes ———

——— A Musician's Journey Through Life and Death ———

——————— PAUL ROBERTSON

FABER & FABER

First published in 2016
by Faber & Faber Limited
Bloomsbury House
74–77 Great Russell Street
London WC1B 3DA
This paperback edition first published in 2017

Typeset by Faber & Faber Limited
Printed and bound by CPI Group (UK) Ltd, Croydon, CR0 4YY

A CIP record for this book
is available from the British Library

ISBN 978-0-571-33190-1

10 9 8 7 6 5 4 3 2 1

To Chika, Thaïs, Caspian and Calista,
and Mum and Dad

Contents

Foreword by Dr Peter Fenwick ————————

What do we mean by 'death'? No respiration, no heartbeat and no brainstem reflexes have long been the clinical criteria of death. The brain in this state cannot maintain consciousness or store memories, so one cannot either experience or remember experiences. This state is known to be irreversible after about five minutes, although by cooling the patient's brain immediately the heart stops, to reduce the brain's need for oxygen, brain function can be restored after up to half an hour without a heartbeat. However, it is known that although consciousness is reversible at this point, this procedure might lead to some degree of brain damage.

But our understanding of the process of dying is challenged when we study the accounts of people who *do* report experiences during cardiac arrest – when their heart has stopped and they have no respiration, no heartbeat and no brainstem reflexes, when they are, in fact, clinically dead. Such experiences are called 'near-death experiences' (NDE). About 10 per cent of all cardiac-arrest patients report fairly detailed phenomena during a near-death experience. Another subset of patients will say they had some experiences during this time. It is now generally accepted that near-death experiences during a profound coma – when there is no heartbeat and to all intents and purposes the patient is clinically dead – can occur. This makes our understanding of the difference between life and death, from a physical point of view, much more complex.

In this fascinating and enormously insightful book Paul Robertson describes what he experienced in the state between life and death. During a lengthy operation to repair a tear in his aorta, Paul was under a general anaesthetic and unconscious. His heart was stopped and his head cooled to prepare his brain for a period of oxygen starvation.

Paul is very clear about what happened to him. While deeply unconscious, he moved from the full awareness that he was dying, to experience of the potential unification of his consciousness with that of the universe: 'As I lay there waiting, I felt myself die – beautifully, ecstatically, transcendently. I saw eternity and shed the whole of myself joyfully in order to become unified with it.'

This is only the beginning of his journey. It is common in near-death experiences for the experiencer to come to a border and realise that if he crosses it he will not return. He might be turned away by relatives who say he still has work to do, or by the Being of Light, the Divine essence of the universe, which sends him back as it is not his time.

Why did Paul, who had seen the transcendent aspect of the universe, its love, its warmth, its bliss, and was doing all he could to join it, decide to come back and rejoin the living? This is not made explicit, but it is evident that he chose voluntarily to return. He describes his return journey in the deepest and most fundamental layers of his mind, up through his psychology, to his final awakening from coma. The understanding that he gained from these experiences of himself and his life, is illuminating for us all. In this book he travels through all the major events of his life and analyses and re-evaluates each of them. One can sense his psychological growth and understanding, his change in maturity, the lessons he has learned and how he has been guided by a universal impulse towards a unity.

Nothing in this state is linear. For time as we know it is different at this level of consciousness. Fragments of Paul's experiences arose, were integrated, only to fall away again and be replaced, maybe by an earlier formative experience, or by a later more major resolution of the causal processes within him which led to the difficulties he had had. He gives insightful accounts of key moments in his musical history, how he met his first violin, how he realised he was musically gifted, how from an early age he saw blocks of his life sketched out in front of him which would lead to a final understanding of musical creativity. His experience while unconscious shows how he stumbled through these, but was always driven to achieve perfection. Few of us can look back on our lives with such insight into our own motivations and how these have led to the successes and failures that we have had. This process is the preparation for death as the ego is cleansed and slowly crumbles, the final freedom.

Throughout this time his wife Chika and his family visited, and Chika continually played CDs she knew were meaningful to him. The family prayed for him and asked him to return, and this was the touchstone that decided him. If there is a 'next time' and he is called 'beautifully, ecstatically, transcendently' to merge with the universe, he will be able to decide to go with the knowledge that his family is reconciled to his decision and can accept his departure.

Soundscapes ————————————————

How I was taken ill and died

One morning at the end of March 2008, as I was shaving in the bathroom of our West Sussex farmhouse, the main artery from my heart ruptured. I felt it snap. Although I didn't realise it at the time, I was dying.

I staggered into the living room, lay down on a sofa and cried out to my eldest daughter. Then I passed out. An ambulance crew arrived and I can remember insisting to them that, although it hurt, the pain wasn't as bad as when I'd had gallstones some months before. I was rushed to hospital, swinging in and out of consciousness.

Many hours later, the registrar told me that since the blood tests confirmed I hadn't had a heart attack I was about to be discharged. Just to be on the safe side he was going to scan my chest. As he was connecting a small device to his laptop, he chatted away with the banter doctors typically employ to distract their patients. He told me he just needed to exclude one rare condition that he had seen only once before. This procedure had previously been carried out by specialist technicians and he apologised for taking so long to get the scanner working. Suddenly he froze, then ran the scanner twice more over an area of my upper chest and commanded me 'not to move on any account'. He made it clear that my situation was 'very critical indeed'. He sprinted off to phone my wife Chika

3

and one of the only two surgeons in the country who could perform the operation I needed.

I went back to drifting gently, as if lying in a punt:

> *Row, row, row your boat,*
> *Gently down the stream.*
> *Merrily, merrily, merrily, merrily,*
> *Life is but a dream.*

The doctor told my wife that my chances of survival were very slim. There was a tear in the wall of the aorta, the major artery carrying oxygenated blood from my heart. At that time, fewer than 3 per cent of patients with this condition survived and most of those that did were left brain-damaged, seriously physically maimed, or both.

Some time later he interrupted my reverie to tell me my wife was on the phone, wanting to speak to me. She was utterly calm and composed as she told me I must now rest as I 'would need all my energy'. I fell instantly into a peaceful deep unconsciousness.

Oblivious of what was happening, I was transferred to St George's Hospital in Tooting, where, by great good fortune, the eminent surgeon mentioned by the registrar had assembled his team. This elite, multidisciplinary group of doctors and nurses had come together on a Sunday in order to try to save me. Thank God for the NHS.

I was briefly roused to find myself lying on a surgical trolley with the team waiting in the next room ready to operate. By now the pain was so intense I could no longer contain it within myself. As Mrs Gradgrind plaintively explains in

Hard Times, 'I think there's a pain somewhere in the room – but I couldn't positively say that I have got it.' All *I* knew was that the whole room was silently screaming with pain.

My youngest daughter lived nearby and a nurse asked me whether I wanted to wait for her to arrive, as the rest of the family wouldn't be able to reach the hospital in time from our home in Sussex. Despite the agony I immediately answered that I did want to wait for her.

For what seemed a very long time I lay there unable to move, longing to pass out. At last I saw her coming through the door. She looked anxious and vulnerable but as beautiful as ever. I remember thinking she was wearing too much make-up and, although I had no idea of the time, I assumed she had been preparing to go out for the evening when the hospital had called. (I later discovered it was still early afternoon.) She came to my side and I could just see her face, although I couldn't seem to move my head. She seemed so unsure of herself – as if she was frightened not only of losing me but also of not being able to find herself. I told her how beautiful she was and reassured her that, blessed with talent as she was, life would certainly bring her everything she wished for. It was a brief but lovely conversation of the sort we never usually afford ourselves in life. A nurse quietly but urgently leant close to my ear and asked me, 'Are you ready to go now?'

Even in such agony the deeper implications of her question were not lost on me and I answered, 'Yes.'

Dying

As I lay there waiting, I felt myself die – beautifully, ecstatically, transcendently. I saw eternity and shed the whole of myself joyfully in order to become unified with it.

During this time I lost all sense of self, including the inner voice normally present within us that tells us who and what we are. That still, small, internal monitoring voice was to remain missing for many weeks. In its absence there were still the sensations of experience, but no 'me' to register them.

Although this state is difficult to describe, it might relate to the feeling of dislocation and confusion that we sometimes experience on waking from a deep sleep. Such detached 'out-of-body' experiences are often associated with severe trauma or dying. In such a condition of 'non-being' there is no sense of time passing so I have no notion of how long I was clinically dead. During much of the spectacular eight-hour operation I was clearly not alive in any ordinary sense.

The doctors opened my chest cavity and then chilled my head in ice in order to slow my metabolism and limit any brain damage. For a critical thirty-four minutes my heart was stopped by administering curare – the South American blow-pipe poison. This stopped all muscle activity while the life-support systems were disengaged and the tear in my aorta could be patched and repaired. During this period my body was 'dead' while my brain was 'hibernating', slowly dying from oxygen deprivation.

As is now the practice following such surgery, I was placed in a medically induced coma for three days, after which the doctors tried to rouse me. Despite their best efforts to bring me round, I remained entirely unresponsive for over three weeks, in a deep coma. Throughout this time I was dreaming strange dreams and seeing visions that were providing me with just enough reason not to surrender to death completely. My mind's attempts to keep me connected to life presented a perception of existence very different from anything usually regarded as 'normal'.

Most of these visions were horrific and some were plainly psychotic. Just one, the very first, was exquisitely beautiful. I found myself worshipping an Asiatic goddess. She was seated, deep in meditation. Her glowing aura of coloured and pure-white light embraced me and other disembodied souls as we floated around her like so many worshipping planets around a sun. Gently, in the background, an unseen woman's voice was singing ravishingly perfect *bhajan*s, Hindu devotional songs.

Towards the end of this extended ecstatic period I began to dare to hope and even anticipate a final permanent state of union with the divine one. This profound longing was accompanied by a kind of accelerated sense of rushing towards total immersion or heavenly 'union'. Suddenly we were surrounded by beautiful, laughing male angels – all dressed in white, clean-shaven, sporting virile swept-back hair and smelling strongly of aftershave (were the nurses at this point shaving me?). But their laughter turned cruel, loud and mocking, because they were actually making sure that none of us souls would ever make the ultimate glorious transition into the afterlife. No, we were destined to remain for ever on the brink: a condition rendered cruelly unbearable because we had glimpsed what would never be ours.

Somehow it was also clear that they were endlessly shitting us out – imagine the torment of knowing that heaven was within reach while being condemned not just to inhabit the lower bowel but actually to *be* the stinking detritus of physical existence.

The meeting place between life and death is like that between the conscious and the unconscious, where experiences are not straightforward but are profoundly mysterious and full of symbols. These states are etched onto my memory in every vivid detail. However, these experiences – like many within music – belong to a richly ambiguous area of human emotion that tends to elude ordinary cognitive categorisation. This might account for such precise recollection being rare and hardly even referenced within medical literature.

Nothing is more ambiguous than the limbo that lies between living and dying. That subtle edge is ephemeral and transient, yet always noumenal. Nothing there, I was to find, is ever simply either happy or sad, rational or intuitive, cognitive or instinctive, but it is always a mixture of these seeming polarities. Things that lie along this cusp might be beautiful and beguiling but they tend to remain ambivalent and paradoxical at the same time.

Meanwhile, in the 'real' world at my bedside, my wife and children were playing me CDs of recordings I had made as leader of the Medici String Quartet. Even though I consistently responded and 'entrained' to the music, I was utterly unaware of 'hearing' it.

On rare occasions I would 'dream' that I was coming closer to consciousness, which felt like attempting to rise up to the surface from deep, achingly cold water. As I 'rose', I recognised elements of my 'self' but the horror of a return to 'life' and what it would involve was too much for me and I would sink back into a profound oblivion. This did not seem in any way to be a choice or an act of will, but rather an automatic reaction from somewhere within the primitive brain areas related to self-preservation and the 'fight or flight' instincts.

In all, seventeen visions or delusional episodes punctuated this extended period of unconsciousness and just a few of them featured the same wonderful microtonal singing as the first.

In one, it was as if I was a 'spiritual teacher' in a stiflingly hot inner sanctum, hoping for enlightenment but secretly fearful of death from the sting of a medicinal snakebite (which might have been a reaction to the sharp but distant jab of a hospital injection). Somewhere out of sight the invisible singer once again quietly sang her consoling songs.

Much later on, while busy being a dog, a husky, in the Arctic tundra, I briefly glimpsed my wife and daughter smiling at me through an apparent rift in the sky. Their presence at that moment seemed an unwarranted and unwelcome intrusion.

Other visions involved feeling nauseous and over-stimulated in the aftermath of a medieval pig slaughter, or lying on the deck of an underwater 'ship of the dead', unable to move.

After I had been in a coma for about nine days, brain scans revealed that I had suffered three strokes and was no longer moving my left side. In some of my visions, including one when I was in New York with Woody Allen watching a television programme featuring a group of dwarfs, I was mysteriously unable to move my limbs. In others I could move freely – swimming underwater at a polluted beach in Cornwall, and so on.

My angelic Indian singer was also briefly present when I seemingly found myself in a New York hospital listening to a man in a nearby bed kvetching and telling jokes in Yiddish to his long-suffering wife or mother.

The dream visions contained all manner of associations and symbols relating to my identity and the nature of the moral qualities that underpin all existence – and every one required later thought and interpretation, some of which I share here.

After such a long unconsciousness, the doctors suggested to my wife that it was now likely that I would never recover and she should consider authorising them to switch off my life support, as they now felt 'there was nothing more that could be done'. Chika, normally a most serene and equable person, was infuriated and took the anaesthetist aside, forcefully insisting that before even contemplating this irrevocable step, 'We could at least pray.'

His reaction was unexpected.

'Yes, indeed,' he said, clearly deeply moved.

'You're right, prayer is very powerful. We must never forget the power of prayer, as it can make all the difference!'

When Chika returned home that late-April night, she found a number of email messages from friends and colleagues telling her that they and other groups had been praying for me that day.

The next morning I awoke.

Miracle or medicine?

Without explanation or preparation I heard Chika's voice, and opened my eyes to discover I was lying in a very odd bed in a strange hospital.

I was also unaware of the drama around me. At the exact moment of my return to consciousness, my blood pressure shot up into the stratosphere, setting off all the monitoring alarms around my bed. Just as I was finding myself so unexpectedly alive, doctors and nurses were rushing to my bedside in the expectation that I was about to die of heart failure.

I wish I could say otherwise, but apart from one instantaneous moment of sheer delight this return to life was in no way enjoyable or joyful. I could not understand what all the fuss was about. I vaguely knew I had been ill, very ill indeed, but I had no immediate understanding that I had been in the underworld for so long. For the first few minutes when I awoke again to the real world, I felt strangely elated but also strangely blank, as if I had just been born. I very quickly discovered that I felt more terribly ill than it seemed possible to be and yet still be alive.

I was also unable to move my limbs. It was fine for my wife and the doctor to smile a lot and speak of a 'miracle', but all I knew was that when I last saw my family I had been a fit, healthy and successful fifty-five-year-old family man with a career that I loved. Now, without explanation, I found myself in intense pain, lying on a hospital bed, completely paralysed down my left side, with a machine breathing for me. It was hard to feel terribly grateful.

As I lay there I saw figures in white – the nurses – scurrying back and forth carrying cups of tea and I became aware of a fearful thirst. We all know what it is to feel thirsty and everyone at some time in their lives will experience dehydration, but this was something else entirely. The desperate craving put me in mind of images of Christ on the Cross, racked with pain.

My wife moistened the tip of a cotton bud to dampen my lips, but like a starving baby I kept catching hold of the little stick with my lips, trying to suck it dry. The senior ICU nurse wouldn't allow any liquid for fear of my coughing and causing damage while I was being ventilated, but at last he relented and allowed Chika to dip some cotton buds in sweet tea for me to suck. Never had anything seemed so lovely. But from then on the whole journey back to life was as disgusting, painful and terrifying as dying had been wonderful and ecstatic.

Shortly after my return to consciousness I was visited by a charming doctor who introduced himself as the anaesthetist at my operation. (He must have been the same doctor who had been persuaded by my wife not to 'turn me off'.) As we conversed and I struggled to breathe, I could see him observing me with a shy fascination. It was only much later that I realised what dedication and skills this fine man must have exercised on my behalf. It was also only in retrospect that I came to discover that following such an extended period in deep coma many patients are irredeemably brain-damaged, so he had naturally come to check me out.

I remember telling him I was a musician and I asked him whether he played an instrument. The sweet man avoided telling me that my chances of ever playing the violin again were remote. Instead he diffidently confided that his young daughter was having lessons.

My wife drew my attention to the patient in the next bed. He had been given a television. To begin with he watched it avidly but as the days went by he slowly became listless and increasingly indifferent. Chika noticed that this poor man never had any visitors and shortly afterwards he disappeared. It seemed obvious to both of us that he had died.

It soon became clear that I was by no means out of the woods myself. Repeated tenacious bouts of pneumonia and many other lung problems resulting from extended dependency on life-support machines, endless blood transfusions and paralysis, the ongoing trauma and gross tissue damage of major heart surgery – none of this makes for a good outcome.

There was also the continuing dependency on morphine and the lasting shock of what had happened to my body, all of which created further confusion and distress. It was perhaps not surprising that I found myself much altered and bewildered.

I kept slipping in and out of delirium and the relative clarity of the first few days was soon replaced by high fevers and hospital-acquired infections, which meant I was constantly being transferred into isolation areas within the ICU. During these days and weeks I experienced recurring bouts of paranoia, panic and episodes of dreadful horror.

On the cusp

For some weeks, I was wandering in and out of consciousness and delirium, and the continual gnawing pain was terrible. For most of this time I was in intensive care. As long as I was on life support I could not communicate how bad I felt – or anything else.

I was prey to strange and confusing delusions. The constant shifting vertigo I was experiencing led me to believe that we were moored offshore in some kind of hospital ship. The nurses and doctors crossing my field of vision were all sailors.

During the periods when I was most ill I seemed to enter a separate reality, a kind of extreme extra-sensory perception in which my carers were revealed in what to me was their psychic totality. I instantly knew when someone compassionate entered the ward, even if I could not see them. Chika was one of these compassionate souls.

One night, I was utterly convinced that the nurses were conspiring to murder me, and was refusing to sleep. I insisted on seeing Chika. The staff begged me not to be so unreasonable, explaining that Chika had been at my bedside all that day and was only now, in the middle of the night, on the two-hour train journey home, exhausted, in order to catch up with her work. (At this time, as well as being a violin professor at the Royal Academy of Music, she was the head of music at a leading public school, which involved organising an extensive freelance staff and the coordination of hundreds of individual weekly lessons.) But I would not be appeased.

After hours of waiting for her return, I psychically recognised that she had at last entered the room next to the ward, and instantly fell asleep. Chika reports having strange waking dreams and psychic visions during her journey. These resolved only as she entered the ICU suite.

Moving hospitals

After I had spent a further month in this twilight world, in mid-May, the decision was taken to move me to a hospital nearer home so that Chika and the family could visit more easily.

The ambulance was hours late. My specialist nurse Matt explains that he and a doctor are to travel with me in the ambulance. I immediately begin to have breathing problems. I am much more frightened about the move than I realise. Matt says he will have a sedative on hand in case the travelling proves distressing but that he expects me to be fine. The journey is terrifying and, to Matt's evident embarrassment, I keep wanting to hold his hand. He tries to distract me by reading aloud articles from the newspaper. The female doctor accompanying us appears disengaged and indifferent, and ignores me.

Once at the new hospital I am immediately surrounded by a team of unfamiliar nurses. They are kind and highly efficient and, after transferring drips and so on, take me through to a single room where a male nurse offers me food and even gives me a menu. It appears to be in French. The overly jolly nurse tries to persuade me to eat, explaining that if I don't he will get into trouble, confiding that this ship has two competing chefs, each determined to murder the other.

The food arrives. It smells wonderful and I realise I am ravenously hungry. But as soon as I've eaten I have the most appalling diarrhoea and am rushed into an intensive care unit where the torture continues.

A new misery is that the bed is too short. Even though I cannot move I am repeatedly drawn down the bed so that my legs are squashed up and cramped at the bottom. I can do nothing to move my legs because they are paralysed. I try to persuade the nurses to pull me back up. I can't speak. Nor can I move anything except for my right hand. They have no comprehension of my pain and distress.

There was nothing wrong with the bed. There was a hand control that raised and lowered the back rest. Desperate to move my limbs, I was constantly pressing the button without realising it. The more I raised and lowered the top end of the bed the further I slid down and the more my legs became entangled with the metal frame.

The horror of choking is ever present. Various devices are used to clear the obstruction. A tube connected to a rubber balloon is inserted into my lungs. A nurse manually deflates and inflates the balloon. It offers some temporary relief from the panic but the sensation is horrible.

Some time later I am taken into the post-stroke ward, a grim place. My family is visiting, along with a kind friend who is a retired professor of medicine. I am terribly ill but perhaps to please my visitors the nurses have propped me up in a chair next to the bed. While I am sitting there the doctor in charge arranges a blood transfusion. It does not hurt but the smell and colour of blood is nauseating. It soon becomes clear I am again running a high fever and even my normally unflappable medical friend looks concerned. As I am being moved back from the stroke ward to the ICU, I see one finger of my left hand slowly bend and then straighten itself. This minute genuflexion is a tiny hopeful beacon.

I receive a visitor and begin recovery

The very first fluttering step on the steep path to recovery occurred while I was still very ill in ICU. I had been there for a few weeks when a close friend, Professor Tony Pinching, the then Associate Dean of the Peninsula Medical School, Cornwall, came to visit.

This medical school was one of the places where I had been teaching after I left the quartet. I spent most of my time travelling the world, lecturing at various universities and business schools. My main topics included the medical humanities, leadership, and the burgeoning study of the musical brain. I invariably used musical metaphor and performance in order to express my ideas.

Earlier that day I had been given an artificial voice box that allowed me to speak in brief gasping whispers. I remember trying to tell this fine man what had been happening to me, particularly the dreams, and desperately grasping his hand for comfort as we spoke.

As an experienced physician, rather than wasting time in commiseration, he told me instead about a recent debate at the medical school between medical ethicists and lawyers on the relative merits of 'correct' legal behaviour versus personal moral conscience, what we might broadly describe as choosing to do the 'right' thing as opposed to merely the 'correct' one.

Although I didn't know it at the time, this distinction had recently been demonstrated, to my advantage, by my anaesthetist's decision to respond sympathetically to my wife's pleas for prayer, rather than to follow the formally 'correct' protocols that would have led to my demise.

While Tony is speaking I can feel my body and mind beginning to draw together for the first time since becoming ill. This is not altogether agreeable as it brings home to me just how disconnected I have become and how sick the neglected parts feel, but it is the first feeling of being 'me' that I've had for a very long time.

I also want to address the paradox of this debate because I recognise that it is exactly the same internal dialogue that has been taking place within me during the visions of my extended 'psychotic' unconsciousness. It is so clear that I immediately begin to gasp out my thoughts.

'The difference is like comparing a good musician to a great one,' I tell him. 'A good performer will faithfully execute the notes of the score as well as he can, but a *great* interpreter such as Murray Perahia transcends such a literal rendition in order to reach the music.' (I have no idea why Perahia's name sprang to my mind – wonderful player though he is and much favoured by my first great musical mentor Clifford Curzon, he was unknown to me personally.)

I go on to explain how this elevated level of performance bears little relationship to the mundane or even the merely talented, for in order to reach it the performer has first to inhabit and then *become* the music. In doing so he remains a faithful servant of the score and yet transcends himself. Though taxing, this peroration leaves me feeling quite a bit better.

Reflecting now about what I said, I can see that it also describes the relationship of our limited personal consciousness, confined as it is to all manner of conventional rules and restrictions, to that infinitely greater encompassing creative consciousness that is the fundamental living force of the whole universe.

Tony listens patiently to my confused and rambling accounts of all the dead people I have recently encountered. As his visit comes to an end, he comments that once I'm feeling a little more recovered I should try to write all this down because it will interest others.

Even during this conversation I am still having strange illusions and keep glimpsing small black animals like turbo-charged squirrels scurrying about the ward and never quite coming into focus.

Also disturbing during this period is my discovery that some of the nurses are actually two-dimensional cardboard cut-outs that exist only in silhouette. I keep checking and, sure enough, many of the nurses never move. I lose consciousness from time to time, but they are always in the same position when I come to again. I conclude this is an attempt to create the impression that the ward is more highly staffed than it actually is. For some reason I find this comforting.

This mistaken but apparently 'lucid' notion was my first fragmented attempt to re-establish my inner 'narrative' voice – a first small step back into a sense of 'myself'. With it came an increasing sense of what was me and what was not me.

After these weeks of immobility, delusion and panic, I finally graduated to an open ward. I was still unable to move my left side and had to be lifted by a hoist on and off the bedpan. I had also acquired deep bedsores, which required regular repositioning of my body in the bed, which was impossible for me to manage on my own. My heart also often went into paroxysms and I could clearly hear and feel it missing beats as I lay there waiting to die.

As time went by a tiny amount of movement became possible in my left foot and physiotherapists visited daily to give me exercises. Even five minutes of effort would throw me into a long exhausted sleep – although sleeping at night was impossible because I would again feel the horrors of my delusional episodes crawling towards me in the darkness.

Some weeks later, in response to my enquiries, a doctor explained that I would almost certainly never walk or play the violin again. By this stage I had pretty much come to terms with the idea of saying farewell to the violin and felt surprisingly at ease with the idea that this was the end of my performing life. In truth, the inability to move myself in bed or even to roll over onto one side was of more immediate urgency. The idea of having to suffer such a 'death in life' and endure the intense pain of paralysis until such time as my body finally gave up – God forbid! – was a truly terrifying prospect.

The doctors, the decent ones at least, were sympathetic but clearly more comfortable with issues they could do something about rather than with the uncertainties of post-stroke care. One evening, having first discreetly checked that no one else might observe him, my delightful cardiologist, Dr Chua, knelt by my side and promised to do everything he could for me. I was touched by his compassion and obvious sincerity. No one spoke about the possibility or implications of dying, nor could I raise this subject even with my wife and children who, perhaps out of concern for my well-being and at least in my presence, seemed to be in total denial. Even so, we all tacitly recognised that my death was an ever present possibility.

On 3 June, after weeks of intense effort, with physiotherapists on each side supporting me, I finally reached the stage of drawing myself upright against a walking frame. The first discovery was that this allowed a view out of the window.

Far off – and what a relief it was to see beyond the windowsill – I could see Chika walking in from the car park. A week or so later it became possible to draw one leg forward, although my limbs seemed to be made of lead. Painstakingly, the physiotherapists encouraged a few faltering steps and after still more weeks of intense effort and nausea, I was able to take a few weak paces unaided.

News of this breakthrough might have prompted the cardiologist to come on his rounds accompanied by a gaggle of junior doctors. They watched my feeble new party trick with amazement and I noticed they all seemed genuinely moved and thrilled to see me doing this. As I finished, I glanced up to find them all smiling, entranced as if full of love and, although I cannot be sure, I think the cardiologist was close to tears.

I prepare to go home

After much debate the consultant began to consider moving me to a rehabilitation hospital. At this time the head of my bed rested against a wall, on the other side of which was an expensive private hospital. As I had private health insurance I enquired whether I might go there instead. Weeks later the insurance company pronounced that 'since I could walk I was clearly no longer sick' and refused to pay out a penny.

It is certainly true that no private medical establishment in this country could possibly have provided the exceptional level of surgical treatment and clinical support I received from the NHS, but the many weeks of recovery spent in a public ward with the aged and infirm in various stages of debility and helpless incontinence were harrowing and profoundly depressing.

I eat an apple

Having lost so much body mass I was constantly hungry. What I most craved were fresh vegetables and fruit, our staple family diet when I was a child. One day I selected an apple from the hospital menu but discovered my jaws were too weak to break the skin, still less bite into it. In the hope of gradually gaining sufficient muscular strength to chew I slowly built up a small collection of apples, which I stored in the bedside cabinet.

About two weeks before returning home it was just about possible to pierce the skin of an apple with my teeth, although chewing more than one small mouthful was still exhausting.

Another indication of progress was the realisation that I was not wearing my wedding ring. My wife brought it to the hospital one day for me to put back on my finger. It had been her father's. He was a conscientious and caring Japanese GP in America who sadly had died too young and long before I met his lovely daughter. I had always felt that his ring carried his love for his youngest daughter and it gives me pleasure to wear it. Even months after the operation my fingers were too wasted to keep it on, so we agreed to make this another goal in my recovery.

Only towards the end of my stay in hospital did I have a few episodes of self-pity – mostly after discovering how much family life I'd missed during my illness. I had been unconscious during my two youngest children's birthdays and was therefore completely unaware that during this time my son had collected a first-class honours degree in economics and my younger daughter had launched an internationally successful pop song.

When I was taken ill I had been an active middle-aged man in the fullness of life but I returned to find myself physically maimed and aged beyond measure.

It took months to accept fully just how ill I had been.

I see myself in the mirror

After months of physiotherapy I was at last able to struggle to the ward toilet all of twenty paces away. Having got there I had to sit down for about ten minutes to recover sufficiently to attempt the journey back. I caught sight of a reflection in the mirror and thought for a moment that some unknown sick old man must have come in with me. My body was appallingly emaciated, my face almost skeletal, and my shoulders, once broad and full, had collapsed. I looked like a starving prisoner of war. The sight of the livid purple scar running down the whole length of my torso was nauseating. It looked as if I'd been savagely eviscerated and, although I'd never been particularly vain, the visible evidence of such a profound physical assault was deeply disturbing. My legs and arms had wasted away from long disuse and my stomach hung like an empty pouch. My head was partially bald and for many months afterwards my hair continued to fall out in clumps.

The shock must have registered on my face. When I was back in bed, an older nurse asked me whether I was all right. As I explained she tutted impatiently, 'Well, of course you look altered, you've just had major heart surgery.' Her indifference was actually very helpful. It was so matter of fact that I couldn't dwell on it. After all, these doctors and nurses were dealing with far worse every day, as were their patients, so who was I to start feeling sorry for myself?

I go home

The consultant suggested yet another move to a hospital specialising in recuperation. However, it soon became clear that this would just put yet more strain on Chika, who had already spent months trying to keep up with her jobs by working through the night. Finally, he proposed that I return home instead, which I finally did in July, four months after my original collapse.

I was duly installed, virtually bedridden, in a small downstairs room. When I arrived home I was some five stone lighter than when I had left. I was still so weak that each day I would have to choose between washing my face or sitting unsupported by the bed for a few minutes, either of which left me utterly exhausted for the rest of the day.

But being at home meant I could gradually begin to creep back into the world. One afternoon, as a treat, our middle child, Caspian, took me around the garden in a wheelchair – something I had longed for during my last months in hospital – but to my confusion and distress, all the flowers I had so much looked forward to enjoying were no longer in bloom and it gradually registered on me that I had missed a whole season. Most of the time I just lay in bed, listening to my heart-beat playing its deadly tango through the pillow.

I watch the builders putting on the wrong roof

Convinced of not being destined to remain alive for very long, I was overcome by a desperate biological urge to provide as well as I could for my family. But my judgement was sadly unreliable. I agreed to pay some rather dodgy builders a large sum of money to mend a roof and was then condemned to watch them using entirely inappropriate tiles to replace the wrong roof. Stuck in bed, there was nothing I could do except lie there and watch the fiasco unfold, for it seemed impossible to communicate my concerns either to them or to my family.

Most of the time I seemed unable to respond or communicate with anyone at all and felt entirely engrossed in my own misery and pain. Just taking the few steps to the toilet without fainting or falling over was a daunting enough task in itself.

Early recovery

Inch by interminably slow inch, I gradually regained some strength. At first, just enough to totter to the next room and collapse in a chair, then, after a while, with great difficulty, to join the family for an occasional meal.

Throughout the rest of that summer I inhabited a grey twilight world. Although I could see the bright sunshine, it seemed strangely unreal and even the wonderfully flamboyant colours of life and nature, which should be so sustaining, became unnatural and tawdry.

On extremely luminous days a weird dark miasma or corona surrounded each vivid image – almost as if the mysterious underlying darkness of the cosmos had become visible and was now revealed like base metal through a worn and shoddy veneer.

For the first few years this altered perception used to frighten me but I have now largely acclimatised to it. As a child I can remember how disconcerting it was when I first saw the moon on a sunny day and it took a similar effort of mind to recognise that this 'darkness at noon' was probably a truer perception into the reality of our manifest universe.

As time passed I also gradually concluded that there was no purpose or reward to be found in staring dismally at the back wall of Plato's cave.

I asked my wife to order Viktor Frankl's book *Man's Search for Meaning*, which I read avidly. While I had always been highly conscious of the horrors of the Nazi death camps, something inside me recognised that now I had spent time somewhere with a parallel quality. Both places were more attuned to death than to life. But now, in order to live, I needed to discern meaning from within this newly subdued monochrome universe.

Frankl's observations of his fellow Auschwitz prisoners led him to conclude that in order to have the *will to live* we must have a sense of *meaning*, which itself comes from retaining some clear *hope for the future*.

I was now living in a pallid grey world, weak and barely able to move, and it seemed imperative for me to construct some aspiration or 'hope'. With little in my mind except end-less reiterations of my recent traumas, I began to write down a detailed account of the dreams and hallucinations that had inhabited my long coma.

Many morbid symptoms remained, including regular periodic sideways 'slips' of consciousness into some other, unpleasantly 'smeared' alternative reality. Although very distinctive, this was extremely difficult to describe. Quite without warning I would find myself inhabiting some other state entirely – one that I instantly recognised but was quite unable to comprehend.

The most disturbing quality of this condition was that as soon as I was within it I could no longer remember my 'ordinary' life in the least. This was so terrifying that I could not move or breathe for fear of becoming stuck there for ever. I concluded that it was probably a symptom of post-traumatic stress disorder (PTSD).

One day as I was standing outside the house, this ghastly shift suddenly hijacked me and I realised that I must assert myself – even at the risk of 'losing' myself entirely. I took one weak step and instantly rediscovered my memories of my wife, family and the daily patina of life.

Nowadays I acknowledge that this fragile and tenuous sense of 'self' is only ever a transitory fabric of pattern and habit. After eight years of intense recollection and interpretation, these hyper-vivid experiences have at last been subsumed into the texture of my 'normal' psychological life.

Sliding doors?

One particular hallucinatory coma sequence seemed to explore this ambiguous nether state.

At the end of one elaborate dream involving a bloody medieval pig slaughter, I found myself standing outside the train station in Twickenham.

Early in our marriage we lived in Twickenham. Oddly enough, even then I was never quite sure whether this station really existed. I used it only once during the five years we were there and could never afterwards work out whether it was as I recalled it or whether I was confusing it with some other half-remembered station. At that period I would occasionally see an attractive young Oriental nanny shepherding two children, whom I assumed were her charges. Every time I saw her I had the same slightly uncanny experience – a kind of 'memory' or knowledge that had I not married my Japanese-American wife I should have ended up married to this girl instead. We never spoke, and as soon as she was out of sight all these thoughts and feelings would be immediately forgotten.

Everything about this dreamlike sequence was deeply ambiguous but my coma vision did make me begin to wonder about the girl I used to see – would she really have been my partner in some other life or was she just sufficiently like my wife to resonate with 'real-life' memories?

Although such partial memories must always remain mysterious, this is another illustration of how one level of consciousness can dominate and overwhelm a separate set of memories.

At some level it seems only too likely that we are all carrying untold wells of such vestigial memory – much of them hardly our own. Music connects directly into this unspoken hinterland and thus allows us evocations of otherwise unexpected aspects of our deepest identity.

Sir John Tavener

Some four or five months after my return to consciousness, towards the end of the summer of 2008, as I was flailing around trying so hard to escape from my febrile state, salvation arrived in the form of a long-delayed handwritten score of a mystical new work composed for me by the leading British composer Sir John Tavener.

Towards Silence is a unique musical depiction of near-death experience (NDE), and the unusual manner of its original commission as well as its auspicious arrival at just this juncture in my life seemed altogether significant.

The first thing that registered was that it was based on a series of Indian classical microtonal *bhajan*s exactly like those I had so recently been hearing within my coma. Furthermore its four movements describe the four principal states of consciousness as defined in traditional Hindu teaching – four states that I had now experienced first hand: *Vaishvanara* is a dense and brilliant restless musical evocation of the 'bright light' of everyday consciousness; *Taijasa* describes the mental activity of the dream-filled sleeping state; *Prajna* is much stiller and explores the deep, joyful healing quality of dreamless sleep, and the final section, *Turiya*, is a gloriously spacious contemplation of the underlying stillness of infinite consciousness – that same darkness that I now see as a necessary corollary of the light.

My first meeting with John

In 1968, when I was a teenager at the Dartington Summer School of Music, there was a memorable early performance of John Tavener's first work to catch public imagination, *The Whale*, based on the biblical Book of Jonah. John was a subject of much popular curiosity at the time as he had been signed by the Beatles for their new Apple record label. *The Whale* was very much a product of its era – the 1960s – and featured performers singing into loudhailers, pre-recorded electronics and other, to use a phrase current at the time, 'way-out' innovations.

It was a particularly hot and sultry summer's evening. As the piece reached its climax with its depiction of a great storm, a massive crash of real thunder ripped and rolled directly above the concert hall. A tremendous storm broke and continued to rage through the rest of the performance, which was all the more memorable because of it.

Going backstage after the concert I found the immensely long and spindly figure of the composer happily folded inside a large wickerwork waste-paper basket, quite unable to remove himself. He looked blissfully cheerful, incoherently waving a bottle of red wine to all and sundry.

The Hidden Treasure

Some twenty years later, towards the end of the 1980s, John composed a work entitled *The Hidden Treasure* for the Medici Quartet. This was written during the same period that he was composing his celebrated cello work for Steven Isserlis, *The*

Protecting Veil, which made a huge impact at the BBC Proms. The piece for string quartet was composed in much the same musical vein, with the composer's unique stamp of static dynamism and developing stillness.

The frequent hallmarks of much post-war classical modernism in music were intellectual structure and an unappetising dissonance. John's mature works are unashamedly spiritual in both essence and intention. He had the rare courage and inner mystical conviction to stick to his chosen path and his quiet certainty gradually attracted a wide and enthusiastic following.

We played *The Hidden Treasure* a great deal and found, as with much of John's music, that it divided audiences into those who could not tolerate what they perceived as repetitive passivity and others who found the work blissful and serene. As a performer I would have to admit to having the same mixture of contradictory reactions within myself.

Towards Silence *is commissioned*

Almost another twenty years later, in 2007, John and I met again at a conference of the Scientific and Medical Network in Bath, when John was the guest speaker and I was commissioned to interview him. In preparation for this I had spoken with him at length beforehand on the telephone.

To my delight I now found him far more approachable and considerably less self-consciously pious. We also discovered a mutual interest in near-death experience, which had long fascinated me.

In the afternoon prior to the evening interview, I was introducing an audience to the hidden Qabalistic numerologies of

Bach's *Chaconne* when the elongated, slightly gaunt and elegant figure of Sir John suddenly made a striking entrance into the church just as I was about to perform. Bach's *Chaconne*, the final movement of his Second Partita, is a profound valedictory 'memorial' to his beloved wife. Although we had no idea at the time, a somewhat parallel destiny was about to play out between the two of us.

After I had finished playing, John and I had a memorable tea with two eminent psychiatrist friends, Peter Fenwick and Andrew Powell, who both specialise in the study of near-death experience. We discussed the sensations, dreams and visions and other powerful altered states experienced by patients who survive clinical death. John was clearly fascinated.

Later that evening, as our interview was drawing to a close, John unexpectedly announced that he wanted me to perform a new work he had long had in mind, an evocation of near-death experience.* It was clear that this bold plan, involving four string quartets and a temple bowl, was no mere momentary whim but already a fully conceived musical idea.

Although the possibility filled me with delight, I felt obliged to remind him that I had left the string quartet some years before. To this he remarked quietly that he thought I 'could do it if I really wanted to'!

Returning home after the conference, I discovered an email from a New York museum inviting me to give a talk about music and spirituality. I spoke with the director by phone that very afternoon and before we had even finished

* This interview, including John's prescient final remark, can be heard on the recording of our conversation at www.soundscapesofthesoul.org.

our conversation he had commissioned John's new piece, with the first performance naturally now scheduled to take place in New York.

I immediately telephoned John, who was clearly terrifically excited and planned to leave for Greece (where he had a home) to compose the work. A few weeks later he called to tell me that the new composition was finished. Being unfamiliar with the way he worked I wasn't sure whether he meant he had actually written it down on paper or merely fully conceived the piece in his mind, but this didn't seem important at the time.

Almost immediately after this conversation we heard that John had collapsed at a concert in Switzerland and was fighting for his life in intensive care. Sometime later, as he lay in a coma, his publishers discovered on his desk an extensive but possibly unfinished manuscript score of the new piece. In the meantime I had already begun programming the first performances and it was while doing so that I too collapsed and was taken to hospital.

Coma vision: in a New York hospital

Exquisite Indian chants also visited an extended coma sequence in which I believed myself to be in a New York hospital – almost as if I was trying to act out being in New York for the first performance of *Towards Silence*, but in an imaginary alternative reality.

Hot and feverish, I cannot avoid overhearing the conversation of a Jewish patient in a nearby bed. I am convinced the doctors are also Jewish – and highly competent. Strangely, all this Jewish ambience does not stop the nurses from decorating the ward for Christmas. There is much discussion about the preparation of food, and giant balloons and large brightly coloured paper decorations are being hung up everywhere. One nurse seems particularly enthusiastic. She constantly hums a mysterious but pleasing little song, always accompanied by a delightful smile. It seems to me that the nurses are not approaching Christmas as a religious festival but are keen to make the atmosphere as joyous as possible.

In intensive care the patient is surrounded by a plethora of devices, many of which hang around the bed. Bells and monitors create a constant mechanised 'musical' narrative. All this, together with the shiny array of clinical and surgical apparatus and bags of blood and serum suspended from wheeled stands, might have given me the impression of a perpetual festive season.

The score of Towards Silence arrives

This arrival of John's score felt to me like a musical augury destined to provide me with a way back into life.

The following day Chika wheeled me into the front room, where for the first time since falling ill I attempted to pick up my violin and bow, which she had lying ready for me to play.

I was so feeble that even lifting the instrument was desperately difficult. Just bringing the violin up to my shoulder was as much as I could manage on that first day. However, I persevered and each day I struggled to achieve just a little more than the day before. After several months I could just about hold the fiddle up long enough to play complete phrases.

Every week throughout this lengthy recovery John and I would speak together on the phone. His intense religious faith prohibited him from complaining, but his suffering was obviously dreadful. We shared a great deal during this time, as perhaps only the intensely sick can share with one another. But beyond the literal horrors of symptoms, doctors and medications, we found ourselves exploring the more abstract issues of life, death and existence.

I found John highly insightful and intuitive. By then his religious beliefs, which I had once found a little overwhelming, had mellowed and broadened into a tranquil and reflective spirituality. My recent experiences had also deflated much of my own judgemental cockiness and so we were able to meet in our mutual no-man's-land.

We agreed, God willing, that we would come together for the first UK performance of *Towards Silence*, which was scheduled in Winchester Cathedral the following year.

Miraculously this came about, and on the day of the concert, recognising how ill John was, the Cathedral authorities compassionately offered to close the building to the public in order for us to have the privilege of playing him an unofficial first performance.

The extraordinary beauty and magic of his unique musical evocation, together with the sight of our dear John and his family sitting quietly alone together in the vast, muted magnificence of this wonderful building, are memories that I hold with deep gratitude.

Following this concert, John and I continued to converse together weekly and even met at his home on the rare occasions I was able to get there. I often scandalised him by insisting that when the time came I would demand an explanation from God for his cruelty in allowing John to suffer as he did. Shocked but moved, he would sigh and cast a loving, long-suffering glance towards his wife Maryanna as she worked quietly in the kitchen, and then his eyes would wistfully stray to their infant son as he played.

John remained at heart a devout Christian, and I a Jewish sceptic, albeit one oddly given to mystical experiences. I was altogether more familiar with dialectical materialism than with piety, so it was odd but wonderful that we found so much to share in those last days.

Learning and performing *Towards Silence* became an extraordinary journey, challenging so many presumptions and assumptions about what music really means. It is also a work of the highest spirituality, ascending step by step from a metaphorical depiction of the 'world' to the most sublime contemplation and a final rich emptiness – silence. The ultimate human spiritual journey.

In performance, the four separate string quartets are placed out of sight of the audience, who are surrounded on all sides by the music. This spacial arrangement creates an experience akin to listening within the womb or a baptism of total auditory immersion rather than that of being in a conventional concert hall. Another strange feature of this performance was that none of the quartets could hear or see the others and, for chamber musicians who never resort to a conductor, this required a huge leap of faith. The result was that the totality of the work transcended any individual virtuosity and built into something far greater than the sum of its parts – very like a devoutly religious life, or a Gothic cathedral.

It also became increasingly clear that – like consciousness itself – the musical truth of the score was revealed by a process of 'stilling' and simplification, like a glass of liquid becoming more translucent as it settles.

Psychologically the piece is a musical testament to the profound insight that 'less is more'. The almost overwhelming over-activity of the opening movement, with its depiction of ordinary life, stands in stark contrast to the intense crystallisation, simplicity and gravitas of its final immovably grounded musical statements, even though study of the score reveals that both are made up of exactly the same musical ideas.

Inevitably, I came to identify closely with John across this time and found myself longing to help him recover. While attempting to adjust to the many limitations of chronic illness myself, I found myself obliged to adopt new strategies in order to provide compensation for the many things I had previously enjoyed but which were now lost for ever. Fortunately, by then, I had discovered the special magic of 'letting go' and was coming to the conclusion that this could be a law of living as well as being a fundamental principle of violin playing. I was desperately praying that the principle that we can only ever 'own' what we have first 'let go' would prove to be universally applicable in life.

John and I discussed this a number of times. Before his final devastating illness he had often composed oblivious of what he was writing, almost as if receiving divine dictation. It seemed to me that, thus transported, he had been experiencing some kind of inspired mediumship. Following his illness and in constant pain, he believed this transcendent state was lost to him. It was not hard for me to identify with this fearfulness, as it is only too natural to lose one's trust following significant trauma and pain. We discussed this together endlessly.

My mum meets John's wife

As John sat propped up in his chair, picking politely at the various tasty morsels we had brought along, Maryanna was describing her studies as a mature medical student in London. Maryanna told us she had been doing anatomy and had recently been dissecting cadavers.

Chika then pointed out that my mother, who had died not long before, had left her body for medical studies to the same hospital where Maryanna was training. Suddenly we all realised that Maryanna had been dissecting my mum's body, a simple enough deduction as there was only one female cadaver. Without anyone referring to it we all glanced anxiously towards John, who fortunately seemed oblivious of this rather grisly turn of events.

The following day Maryanna called to tell us that one of John's works had just been performed at a memorial service held by the hospital to honour those such as my mum who had left their bodies to medical science.

Scatter Roses

As John continued to suffer the inevitable progress of his illness, I urged him to listen again to the late Beethoven quartets, which I am convinced are the glorious product of just such abject personal loss. John admitted to having had reservations about these great works, considering them too expressive of human suffering.

Imagine my delight when John telephoned me to say that he had succeeded in finishing a short quartet movement, *Scatter Roses Over My Tears* (a quotation from one of Rumi's most lovely poems), based on both the 'Hymn of Thanksgiving on the recovery from illness' from Beethoven's Op. 132 and the wonderfully detached slow movement of the final quartet, Op. 135.

The Medici Quartet had the enormous pleasure and privilege of premiering this lovely work but alas, not to John himself, for by then his years of suffering were over.

Learning and playing this final quartet movement of John's taught me at least two significant things. First, I discovered that the composition was a perfect palindrome (reading the same backwards as it does forwards). This was a small but significant revelation to me as I suddenly understood how it was that John's music could so often embrace both development and stasis. When I mentioned this at the first performance Maryanna confided that 'actually all of John's mature pieces are palindromic'.

For readers who might be unfamiliar with such musical symmetries, I should explain that the structure of John's works are in no way formulaic. For example, while the actual pattern of notes might be reversed across a phrase, melody, movement or complete work, there will be other rhythmic or note-length symmetries occurring at the same time. This means that although the patterns can be inferred or 'sensed', they can be surprisingly tricky to identify.

In this Tavener is applying very similar principles as such mighty figures as J. S. Bach and Arnold Schoenberg, who were also compulsive mathematical manipulators within their compositions.

It is interesting to speculate whether such 'pattern making' is an inherent expression of how the brain functions in its neuronal firing. Nor are these design applications culturally specific. Admirers of Islamic art will observe exactly similar subtle reversing symmetries in carpet weaving as well as in more explicitly religious design and ornamentation.

It only gradually dawned on me that the psychological structure of *Towards Silence* is also a beautiful living demonstration of the subtle interwoven hierarchies of consciousness; in particular that each and every level of ourselves is capable of encompassing and enveloping the others, assuming a temporary dominance. This why we tend to assume that each successive current aspect of ourselves is the totality of who we are.

Certain music reveals this enveloping partiality to startling effect. To me Schubert is a prime example of this. So often each of his successive miraculous melodies moves us so powerfully that we find ourselves inwardly convinced that it is only *now*, in this present instant, that the music has truly begun. A few moments later we experience exactly the same sensation all over again in his next melodic ravishment – but even more so! Although I would not ordinarily associate the music of Schubert and Tavener, both demand that we stay in the present moment.

I am taken ill again

Over the two-year period of performing this life-giving work, I finally regained enough confidence to risk accepting an invitation to attend a conference in Athens with the European Cultural Parliament. This was wonderful but risky and, having alarmed my hosts by passing out in the central hall of the Greek parliament building, I returned home only to fall back into a pattern of increasingly nightmarish semi-comas.

Although I tried to deny it to myself, my breathing was again becoming increasingly distressed and I had to return to hospital. I was also suffering constant vertigo and it soon became clear that this was the result of an irregular heartbeat, an atrial fibrillation which had caused blood clots (pulmonary emboli) to form in my lungs. These clots are very dangerous – in the brain they can also cause devastating strokes – and I was therefore kept under observation in hospital for a few days while blood thinners were administered.

The main symptom of this condition was an inability to think or feel normally. My mind felt as if it was forever slipping sideways into a horrible 'smeared' place where it was impossible to exercise any control over my sickly imaginings. The most disturbing part of these symptoms was that I could no longer use my mind in order to recollect my sense of self. I found it unbearable to imagine dying in such a confused state.

However, it was obvious that others around me were even worse off. The unfortunate man in the next bed, only a couple of feet away, was suffering far more and did not even have any privacy. In the middle of the night he received the grim news that his cancer had metastasised throughout his body and he now had only two or three weeks to live. He was unable to tolerate morphine-based opiates, and even his examination was almost too appalling to contemplate. The sympathetic doctor was clearly mortified and begged his forgiveness for the pain she was causing him. All of this was sobering and inescapable.

I think this incident finally brought home to me the vital necessity of establishing a *cognitive* understanding of what dying was going to mean to me. It is one thing to experience the trauma of dying but quite another truly to come to terms with one's own mortality. There has always been a two-year periodicity in my life, by which I mean that it usually seems to take about two years before my intentions reach fruition. Now, it was also to take two years to affect this particular significant change of attitude.

I sell my violin

Once the Tavener performances had run their course about two years later, I realised that it was time to give up my beautiful eighteenth-century Italian violin, made in Venice by Dominicus Montagnana in 1729.

This decision represented a very significant psychological shift to me because, even though I still hoped to be able to play some other violin for my own consolation, it had become evident that I didn't need to own such a priceless instrument nearly as much as my family needed the money to live on.

Chika generously and courageously made the same choice and also reconciled herself to parting with her own lovely old Italian violin, a quirky instrument made by Paolo Antonio Testore in 1720 that I had used earlier in my career. So we set about selling them both.

To me, playing the violin was never just a career choice but for all sorts of reasons the central core of my existence: it was my closest friend, confidant, comrade and lover. Above all it was also the fullest expression of myself – of who and what I was. The actual instrument itself acted as my constant talisman against everything that was terrifying in 'real' life – particularly my own mortality. The violin and my intimate relationship with it constituted the only aspect of my existence I was fully able to trust.

This arose because of various events throughout my life, particularly during my earliest childhood. Certain key early experiences form the basis of our human psychology and personal identity, but it is doubtful that we can actually *choose* any of these seminal occurrences. When we come down to it, we have no choice but to live the life we have been given.

For most of us the objects that come to invest our lives with meaning seem to appear by chance, happenstance or upbringing. There might be certain developmental windows or key moments when we are primed to establish specific associations and bonds. But this is not how we experience it subjectively.

When we are young and still 'trailing clouds of glory' as Wordsworth has it, certain events apparently arrive almost magically or with such an overwhelming synchronicity or enhanced consciousness that they continue to inform everything that follows.

The first of these moments in my own life occurred when I was very young and we were living hand to mouth in a caravan by the River Thames in Kennington, on the outskirts of Oxford . . .*

* Some fifty years later when I was awarded an Honorary Fellowship to Oxford's Green Templeton College, as I was giving my inaugural speech it dawned on me that the hall where I was speaking was no more than two or three hundred yards away from this caravan site where I had spent my early childhood.

That my father was in love with my mother is beyond doubt. When they first met at the beginning of the war she was, according to them both, vivacious, attractive and bubbly, and he was – literally – a tramp, living rough because his passionate adherence to socialism had led him to repudiate both the capitalist system and militarism.

When he was arrested for ignoring his military call-up, he read the court a carefully prepared and highly principled Marxist rebuttal, which meant he spent the rest of the war on the run from the police and the military authorities.

As socialists, Mum and Dad also spurned the institution of marriage, finally tying the knot only in order for me not to have 'illegitimate' stamped on my birth certificate.

I was about three years old when Mum used to take me to a kindergarten in Oxford, near Morrell's brewery with its overwhelmingly heady and sickly smell of hops. One teacher there was often impatient when I got confused about how to put on my coat or was slow doing up my shoelaces. This teacher's hands and voice became rough and angry when I struggled with these simple tasks and she spoke rudely to my mother about how 'undeveloped' I was, although I never seemed to have these problems except with this particular teacher.

Later on, I realised that my mother suffered similar lateral confusion and disorganised functioning, because being naturally left-handed she had been obliged throughout her childhood to act as if she were right-handed. As a result, when stressed, she would panic and become dreadfully self-conscious about what she called her 'cack-handedness'.

At the nursery school we were all 'set down' on little mattresses for our afternoon nap. On one occasion, instead of instantly dropping off to sleep as usual, I found myself strangely wide awake and self-aware. I raised my head and, sure enough, everyone else was fast asleep. Suddenly I comprehended that *I was awake*, watching them!

Even now I can recall the deep thrill this awareness gave me. It made me feel profoundly different from everyone else because this new kind of 'consciousness'* made me see that other people were mostly *not* aware of themselves.

I promised myself to sustain and cultivate this strangely attractive state, but of course when I awoke it was completely gone and forgotten. This wonderful feeling of separateness and superiority was my first taste of what I now consider to be a rather unusual recursive 'self-consciousness', which was to become my default mode whenever I was under pressure.

It was an aspect of performing that I found highly attractive. The scintillating yet modest violinist Fritz Kreisler also seems to have known its allure: strolling past a fish shop in New York with a friend and spotting rows of codfish with their open mouths and glazed eyes, he famously remarked, 'Oh, that reminds me. I have a recital tonight!'

Mum always insisted that when they first met she had found Dad singularly underwhelming, particularly as his opening gambit was to ask her to sew a button onto his coat. Curiously enough, she had already enjoyed another significant relationship with a tramp earlier in her life. Back then

* The esotericist and Gurdjieff disciple P. D. Ouspensky describes such heightened self-awareness as 'self-remembering'.

it was a hapless vagrant whom her kindly father had invited home for Shabbat. This desperately quiet young man was then invited to stay and clean the house in exchange for board and lodging.

My mother was brought up in the East End of London. There were eight or nine children sleeping in two beds. Her mother was in the grip of constant depression and her loving rabbinical father had no choice but to run a sweat-shop tailoring business employing his own children.

Since my grandmother had long since abandoned any attempt at housekeeping, my mother took to getting up at five each morning to clean the house. When the new lodger moved in, sleeping in the broom cupboard under the stairs, they used to get up together to clean. This went on for many months. He said very little, although it was quite clear to her that he was a caring and educated man.

Much later, my mother's older sister discovered that he was none other than Eric Blair (aka George Orwell). At that time he would have been researching *Down and Out in Paris and London*.

Fortunately love knows no bounds and dear Dad, indefatigable Geordie that he was, pursued her remorselessly. I suspect she saw in him someone both intelligent and kind, as was her own affectionate father. Dad was an autodidact and could turn his fine, perceptive mind to whatever he felt was worthwhile or necessary. Their early years together were spent in a caravan and my mother always insisted that it was her happiest time of her life.

When I was about six years old, we moved out of our tiny caravan into a little two-up two-down terraced house in

Oxford's Cowley Road and I attended the local East Oxford Primary School.

My first musical experience: 'The Cuckoo'

My first musical experience occurred when I was about five. For some reason our usual teacher was away and a rather nervous supply teacher came in to give us a music lesson.

Despite sitting at the grand piano in the main school hall, she begins by apologising for not being able to play it. We are all sitting on the wooden floor, which I dislike because it is so uncomfortable – dry, dusty and full of splinters.

The teacher starts to sing a little song which is new to me, 'The Cuckoo'. 'Ta, ta ta ta ta tilah. Cuck-oo,' she sings, hesitantly contriving at the same time to play the simple melody on the piano. When, with difficulty, she reaches the 'Cuck-oo' she even manages to pick out the cuckoo's call, harmonised in pleasing thirds.

I raise my hand. 'Yes?' she enquires kindly. I explain shyly that I need to go to the toilet. 'Yes, of course, dear,' she says, and I toddle off.

When I return the song is still in full flow. 'Ta, ta ta ta ta tilah. Cuck-oo,' she sings. By now, she hardly has to slow up to play the two consecutive thirds. To my surprise I find I need to go to the toilet again. She looks a bit disconcerted but I have the face of an angel and am clearly not making it up.

This time when I get to the toilet I find that although I have a funny feeling in my willy I cannot pass any water. Puzzled, I wash my hands and go back into the hall where yet another verse is in progress.

'Ta, ta ta ta ta tilah. Cuck-oo.' Sure enough, as the two fall-ing thirds sound again I get that funny feeling of needing to go to the toilet. Slightly awkwardly this time, I raise my hand once more. The teacher now looks at me very keenly and asks the class whether Paul is normally a good boy. He is, they assure her. With the injunction to 'be quick then' I retrace my steps to the toilet. This time there is definitely something very odd about my willy. It is all stiff and hot and there is simply no way I can persuade it to go to the toilet.

Feeling quite confused, I go back into the lesson where every time the 'Cuck-oo' sounds I have the same strange sensation — but by then I realise there's no point going to the toilet.

Psychiatrists tell me that this kind of pre-adolescent sexual arousal can sometimes be associated with epileptic seizures leading to adult sexual fetishism, fixated on the particular object or activity associated with its first occurrence. How-ever, while it is certainly true that much of my later activity and sexual identity was oriented by music, and particularly the violin, I have never been epileptic.

How then do I account for this curious sequence of events? The easy answer is that I don't. If we are honest about it there are many such events in life that defy our ordinary rational understanding.

Unsurprisingly perhaps, this selfsame cuckoo (or its close cousin) had a cameo role in one of my coma visions.

My parents' relationship

As I grew a little older I could not help being aware that my parents did not have a perfectly happy marriage.

48

Unfortunately Mum's fundamental practicality and early hardships had left her keenly suspicious and cynical. Kindly men she dismissed as 'stupid', while intellectual idealists were labelled not only as 'stupid' but 'weak' as well. Dad fell into both categories. However, neither judgement stopped her, even in the same breath, from acknowledging his exceptional intelligence, decency and kindness.

In my youth I couldn't help sharing her view, at least to some extent. Much as I loved and admired my father's high-minded Marxism – which sometimes involved standing on a soapbox in the Cornmarket, Oxford, preaching the abolition of the financial system and a new order of enlightened humanity – I could not help noticing, his cronies apart, that no one else took his views remotely seriously. After a while it also began to strike me that the various intense 'comrades' who came round each week to harangue each other were probably there only because of his intellectual and moral courage.

Mum was brutally uncompromising in her judgement. These dialectical debates always seemed to finish rather late and involve much drinking of tea and passing of political tracts. As she was running around clearing up afterwards she would invariably remark, 'So, how does it feel being Jesus Christ? Have you and your cronies sorted out the world yet?' Still flushed with heady intellectualism, my dad would never fail to rise to this ultimate insult and launch into another lengthy socialist rationale.

However, they were both of one mind when it came to religion, which was something they scornfully dismissed. Indeed, Dad insisted on calling Jesus Christ 'Jim', which always made me cringe. Whatever Christ had been, I couldn't help feeling this was deeply wrong. Not that I was a believer; at the age of about seven I had dared to lift my head during school prayers and felt surprisingly relieved not to be one of the herd.

It is one thing not to be conventionally devout but quite another to deny any spiritual existence altogether.

Dad finally took the plunge and resigned his job as the manager and general accountant of a hire-car company, and started his own business – an employment agency, which he ran from our front room. Almost immediately after this he began to suffer chest pains, and just as the business was beginning to get off the ground he had a full-blown heart attack. He was in hospital a long time and although I didn't understand much of what was happening (I was eight at the time), I did appreciate that most of his new 'friends' in the ward were dying off one by one.

From then on my poor dad was beset with the savage agonies of angina. His walking became halting and effortful, but, sweet man that he was, he never complained and always retained his essential engagement with the world of ideas and radical left-wing politics. He just battled on, often in frightful pain, gradually adapting to life as an invalid, yet still somehow managing to grow his business. This was long before 'stenting' became possible and I suspect that nowadays his condition would have been corrected relatively easily.

As his upper body and face became twisted by chronic pain he developed a shambling gait. Although unaware of it, I assumed exactly the same hesitancy and wounded manner of walking. This physical empathy was my childish way of showing him love. Such physiological and emotional mirroring was my primary emotional language, as it probably is for most children and all naturally gifted and intuitive instrumentalists. Nowadays, neuroscientists speak of mirror neurons,* which I have no doubt are implicated in such unconscious imitation.

Darkness and dread

From this time onwards I was beset with a sense of nameless horror, which took the form of a pit gaping open at my feet. This appalling underworld was filled with rotting dead bodies, distorted limbs and writhing, suppurating cadavers. Although I dedicated my every waking moment to avoiding this abomination I could never fully escape it.

One day on my way to school – compulsively reading as I walked – this ghastly pit nearly swallowed me up. There on the edge of the pavement I suddenly lurched downwards, my legs nightmarishly entangled with the skeletal limbs of the dead.

I concluded that only constant hyper-vigilance could save me from this dreadful netherworld. This watchfulness served a dual purpose: firmly detaching me from all unnecessary 'sentimental emotion' while charging me with obsessional energy to pursue alternative creative distractions.

I sustained this vigilance even when my beloved father died, and again when Mum departed. I shed no tears for either. Although I was surprised to find myself momentarily welling up when I took our little cat Alice to be put down – she

---

* Mirror neurons fire up both when we perform a particular action and when we observe the same action being performed by someone else and are part of a highly complex mechanism involving many brain areas by which our own brain physically mirrors others.

was so clearly suffering and yet still continually and valiantly attempted to lift her face towards the sunlight.

So compulsive was this neurosis that I never took a holiday or gave myself a day off. I was unconsciously certain that the death pit was always waiting for just such an opportunity.

This universal background darkness is the black corona of light without which there is no colour and the pure emptiness of that absolute silence on which only the purest sounds can be etched.* From the time it emerged I dedicated all my energy and attention only to such activities that could use this surrounding 'nothingness' to enhance life: the violin, imaginative literature, beauty, esoteric philosophy and so on – all activities that become intensified by contrast with the blackness.

At a later stage this same darkness took to clothing itself in diabolical forms, for instance when Manoug Parikian (see p. 75) died, and again when I was so cruelly returned to life. More recently it has assumed the shape of the formless horrors of dying in the sickly night-time.

'Valence' is a term often applied to the shifting emotional states mediated by music. At the 'affective' level heightened emotion and arousal is clearly magnified when placed against a subdued or 'flat' field.

In much the same way that I would find myself suddenly marooned in some alternate wakefulness following my coma, the miseries of heart failure now reveal how utterly terrifying it is to let go of a waking state and fall asleep – the metaphor of death is simply too immediate.

* It can be clearly heard on some of the very greatest early violin recordings by Heifetz and Menuhin and so forth.

Music can still carry me over with a loving hand – but when alone, as the forms of life and mind grow unstructured and begin to melt, the childlike terror without form, and pain divorced from feeling, are simply too terrible to contemplate.

Just as personal joy can extend into a universal ecstasy, there is an obverse symmetry in which seemingly subjective suffering can open a vortex – even into the horrors of the extermination camps.

Perhaps neither positive nor negative emotional states can be claimed or owned. They are never 'ours' – but merely exist as the polarities of the human soul.

The fact that just beyond the bleak bereft *Beklemmt** place stands a host of loving friends ready to welcome me as yet still does not seem certain enough, even though I know they are constantly there.

Making ends meet

Following Dad's heart attack the spectre of penury once again stalked the house. Mum was obliged to become his carer, which was never going to be an easy role for her. She was an energetic, athletic person and now found herself constantly having to adjust to Dad's tediously slow pace, forever running ahead then feeling guilty and turning back to him. I now observe all this being recapitulated in my own life and resent it terribly.

From this time on my mother's incipient anxiety became rampant. The scatterbrained, fun-loving girl she always

* For Beethoven's telling use of the marking *Beklemmt* in his Op. 130, see p. 204.

insisted she really was became increasingly subsumed into a hysterically nagging virago. Never given to reflection and in the grip of her inner fears, she was capable of saying the cruellest things. Trying to keep pace with the bills, she spent days and nights sewing on a little Singer treadle sewing-machine. The more desperate things became, the more she sewed, but not surprisingly the more anxious she was the less efficiently she functioned.

One afternoon, when I was about seven, I was sitting miserably in the corner of our ramshackle outhouse watching her sew. I heard her gasp and suddenly hunch over the machine uttering some terrible profanity. In her haste and exhaustion she had sewn completely through all her fingers. Carefully rolling back the spindle of the machine so that the needle finally withdrew, she used her other hand to cut herself free. This allowed her to withdraw the injured hand, which still had threads running through it. She bit them off and drew them out one by one, hastily wrapped a piece of scrap material around her fingers, and just went on sewing. Accidents like this became a regular occurrence.

It was at this critical and unhappy juncture that I discovered my true calling.

My first violin lesson

When I was eight years old, the school gave us all a letter to take home offering a term's free recorder or violin lessons. I was duly packed off by my impoverished parents to learn the violin. There was an inevitability about this choice; my mum being Jewish and both my parents being music lovers, the

54

offer of something culturally enlightened and cost-free was irresistible.

For reasons I cannot now recall I missed the first few weeks of tuition but was finally fished out from class and sent along, full of trepidation, to a distant classroom for something called a violin lesson. I had no idea what a violin was and the tortured sounds emanating from behind the door of this unfamiliar room did not augur well. However, I plucked up my courage and grasped the door handle.

As soon as my hand neared the handle, a strange and powerful feeling overcame me and I began experiencing an overwhelming feeling of déjà vu, which continued as I crept into the room and persisted throughout the ensuing lesson.

At the front of the classroom a funny little man stands pulling faces at a group of bemused children. Under his chin he holds a violin and with his other hand he is waving a curious stick – the bow. He beckons me in, saying, 'I don't know why you've missed so much of the term and it's too late to catch up but you might as well listen since you're here now', and continues teaching the other kids. He is playing scales and then pausing theatrically before introducing a grotesquely out-of-tune wrong note. To make his offence inescapably obvious he simultaneously pulls a comically exaggerated, horrified face.

He then patiently asks each child in turn whether this offending note sounds right or wrong. To my mystification the children reply one after the other that what he's playing sounds fine. He sees me looking shocked and invites my opinion. 'It's quite wrong,' I reply. He looks relieved and says, 'Well, at least you've got an ear.' Since this seems incontrovertible, I say nothing.

He then starts asking the pupils to come up one by one to the front of the class and 'draw a straight bow' (a single long note on the open A-string). Seeing me watching intently he invites me to try too.

The violin feels very lumpy under my chin but as soon as the bow is in my hand everything seems curiously familiar and comfortable. I am dimly aware of his voice continuing to give instructions and when the bow starts to draw a sound from the string I am entering a powerfully personal world.

By halfway along the bow's journey I recognise that I am a violinist and during the last half of the bow stroke I am planning out my future life in detail. This entails needing to work single-mindedly until the age of twenty-five, which is when I shall at last be able to produce the sound I really want to.

I also make an internal compact with myself that if I devote myself to being the very best violinist I can be until the age of forty-two, I shall then give myself permission to explore any other areas of life that interest me. I feel sure that, by then, music will have given me all the insights I need in order to undertake any other discipline or skill. When I get home that evening I announce to my parents that I am a violinist.

I have tested this memory many times during my life. To the very best of my knowledge I had never even seen a violin before this lesson and didn't even know what a violin was. As to the impact of having such an extended déjà vu, years of sceptical investigation have left me content to accept P. D. Ouspensky's theory that such 'memories' probably represent an emotionally enriched reiteration, not so much of a previous life but of the one we are living now, but experienced at such an enhanced level of intensity and depth that time and space shift into an entirely new relationship.

If this is true, it marks out such a life event as belonging to a similar class of experience to that of falling in love at first sight, which also cannot easily be rationalised or explained away. Exactly why and how so many people receive an immediate intuitive understanding of something that is to become so important in their lives remains fascinating and elusive.

Along with this new-found sense of myself and my destiny, a number of other 'facts' made themselves known. Among them was the complete certainty that as long as I stuck to the violin I would never have to search for anything elsewhere. In other words, the world, and any help I might need, or remarkable people I might need to meet, would all *come to me*.

At this early age I also felt a strong desire to experience absolutely everything that I would need to, in order not to have to return to an earthly existence again. This might sound a little unusual but has remained a prevalent feeling. (It might also be some indication of just how much I disliked my life at this unhappy period.)

The fuller implications of this strange aspiration became clearer only after I was ill. After all, to have experienced everything that life can bring is not for the faint-hearted and probably not entirely wise.

Another interpretation might be to regard all these events as self-fulfilling. Maybe I did not become a violinist *because* of my apparent memory of already having been one, but because the power and energy of the event itself gave me sufficient emotional impetus to sustain all the work that made it come true.

Cause and effect become very confused at this level. Having spent many years thinking about it I suggest that the principle of Occam's razor demands that we take seriously the possibility that an event can be valid in itself. Maybe we experience a feeling of prescience because that is exactly what it is.

In some inexplicable way the unconscious anticipation of meeting the violin primed me to fall in love with it. Is falling in love at first sight with a violin a miracle? It is certainly unusual but surely so is 'falling in love' in any context.

It was certainly my great good fortune that in my case the object of my obsession was something as benign as the violin because music has the capacity to lift us to the highest creative energies of the universe and in doing so obliges us to seek our most noble possibilities.

I was also blessed by having a father who always took my singular aspiration entirely seriously. I would often hear my mother's anxious voice questioning the wisdom of my wanting to become a violinist. 'How will he end up?' she would demand rhetorically. Then she would answer her own question: 'Desperately begging under the arches at Charing Cross station like all the others.'

Then my father's gentle voice would answer saying, 'No, no, there is nothing more precious in life than to discover what you love' – he would know, poor soul! – 'and *then* once you do there is nothing more important than to pursue what you love *throughout life*.'

I was indeed fortunate to have such an enlightened father and he was as good as his word, supporting me with all his affection throughout my early career.

However, life has also taught me some other lessons since then. One is that although we fall in love with the *object* of our desire, only very gradually do we come to realise that this object is actually partially a projection of our own longings. The powers of 'love' are not necessarily connected in the way we think they are.

The greatest musicians remain in love with their instruments throughout their lives, sometimes almost narcissistically, but the best of them never cease to give off and experience an aura of lightness and affection, love and joy.

Yet not all love is equal: nothing is more grotesque and pathetic than old men who remains pathetically attached to an essentially youthful desire for feminine beauty. There are 'right' and 'wrong' times for all human desire and any over-attachment or fixation can turn a gift into a hurdle.

One of my heroes, the Sufi master Hazrat Inayat Khan, became a master musician at an early age. He describes his progress as being at first a *devotion* to music and then discovering that people actually came to listen to him because of the love he conveyed *through* his music. Finally he realised that he no longer needed an instrument in his hands to shape and heal his listeners' souls and so gave up musical performance altogether.

Of course it is a rare privilege for any of us to be able to *do* what we *love*. But in the end the bigger lesson is to learn how to *love* what you *do*. The first gives us a vocation and reason to live but the second offers freedom. Perhaps the ultimate gift of illness lies in the obligation it places on us to learn first-hand how to extend such feelings of love to whatever is left with us as we go.

Fortunately all human beings are granted glimpses of this when they fall in love and discover that the greatest gift of ourselves is to another person (or object) when we experience that divine gift: 'in whose service is perfect freedom'. This exactly describes the gift of music and its lovely embodiment in the instrument of the violin as it came to me.

Nothing about this fundamental feeling has changed throughout my lifetime, but now I realise that my appreciation of it was first *personal*, then *relational* and finally a metaphor of the *transcendent*.

Instrumental empathy

As time went by I learned to 'read' other violinists through the gestures of their playing. Once I had heard or seen someone play the violin I knew everything about them, their nature, personality, nobility and integrity – or lack of it. Later on, I realised that I only ever became seriously involved with girls whom I had seen playing the violin.

I don't think this was any kind of fetish but merely my own way of understanding other people's true nature. As soon as I saw someone playing the violin they became totally transparent to me. I felt safe and in control, so perhaps it is not surprising that I also tended to trust myself sufficiently to find female violinists strangely erotic. This ability to 'read' people through their playing became so familiar that I came to regard it as entirely normal and still do.

I should point out that it is probable that we all have similar gifts but applied in accord with our situation and upbringing.

Interpreting musical personalities

Although lacking any formal musical education and undoubtedly hard up, my parents were altogether supportive of my musical aspirations. Dad even bought a little radio for my bedside and tuned it to the Third Programme (BBC's classical music programme, the forerunner of Radio 3) so that I woke to the sound of fine musicians performing and drifted off to sleep each night in their company.

In this way I became something of a connoisseur of the great players of that era: Kreisler, Menuhin, Szeryng, Milstein, Oistrakh, Szigeti, Heifetz et al. Without knowing how or why, I came to recognise the nature and personality of these great violinists from their playing.

Yehudi Menuhin's almost painful vulnerability and emotional honesty was always compelling, whereas the dazzling and flawless Henryk Szeryng never commanded such total emotional engagement. David Oistrakh's playing was great, noble and always generous, while Fritz Kreisler constantly stirred my heart with his gentle touch – and because of this I loved him most of all.

Some years later, when I won a scholarship to the Royal Academy of Music, there was much debate as to why I played with such a distinctively small and hissy sound. The answer was actually simple. It was because I was unconsciously replicating Kreisler's playing as I had first heard it recorded on early 78 rpm discs, heard over a small transistor radio.

Szigeti was a player whose lucid mind I also found deeply attractive. I particularly loved his 1935 recording of Prokofiev's First Concerto with Sir Thomas Beecham, which felt like a wonderful Platonic dialogue. In time this was to become my own path. Years later I discovered that Szigeti had also significantly influenced and been a close friend of my musical hero, Clifford Curzon.

However, arguably the greatest player of them all created an uncomfortable ambivalence in me. The daunting Jascha Heifetz with his thrilling sound and sheer willpower was at once overwhelming, exhilarating and slightly frightening. I admired him, as we all did, but had no desire to imitate him in my own playing, although I did learn a lot from him – both good and bad.

Mozart wins the pools

After a term, my allocation of free violin lessons from the school ceased, leaving my parents obliged to pay for private lessons with my beloved first violin teacher, Gilly (Mr Gilette-Smith). Financially, this was no small matter.

Despite his health problems, Dad had by then managed to create enough success in his burgeoning business to buy a small van and it was his pride and joy. Cowley Road, where we lived in our little terraced house, was the main thoroughfare for the vast workforce who slaved on the assembly lines at the massive BMC motor works.

At exactly 5 p.m. each afternoon I would watch a sorry torrent of exhausted, white-faced men cycling slowly past at the end of their gruelling twelve-hour shift. They looked like the living dead and as such might well have revisited me in my later coma visions. It wasn't until years later that any of these industrial wage-slaves were earning enough to drive their own cars and it was therefore no small achievement for Dad to have become a car owner so early on.

We used to go out for family trips, mostly to visit my dad's sister and her family or his brother Andrew, who were the only relatives who remained available to us. But one day the little white van mysteriously disappeared. Dad was careful to say nothing about it but Mum made a point of telling me how much he had sacrificed for me, as it was now paying for my violin lessons.

Until then I had been borrowing a typical school violin, referred to as 'the box', but as I remained enthusiastic and was developing so quickly, my violin teacher Gilly became bent on persuading my parents that it was time I had a better and much more expensive fiddle. With this in mind he kept on mentioning a violin-maker he thought very highly of, Arthur Richardson, of Crediton in Devon. But the instruments he made cost a princely £80 and there was simply no way it was possible for my parents to afford that much.

At this time most working people did the football pools in much the same way as everyone does the lottery today. This involved filling in columns on a coupon in order to predict which teams would draw their matches that week. Dad 'invested' about sixpence a week on this relatively benign gamble. Dad's father had devoted nearly forty years of his life to perfecting a statistical analysis that he believed would finally guarantee success in winning the pools. His system consisted of meticulous notes recording the teams' past history over many years when playing each other. The fact that he never succeeded in beating the odds was, he insisted, because the continuity of the teams' performances had been disrupted by the Second World War.

On the rare occasions we visited Grandad he would give Dad lengthy demonstrations of this harmless eccentricity, but my father was sufficiently mathematically savvy not to fall for such illusions. He already had a host of idiosyncratic beliefs of his own, but he also felt there was nothing to lose by filling in the coupons.

Because of the violin drama, Dad suggested I be allowed to select our prediction for drawn matches that week. By then my only coherent world was the violin, so in order to comply I created a system with which to convert the notes of the Mozart concerto I was learning into a numerical sequence to apply to the code number identifying the matches on the coupon – quite unaware that such numerology was based on the Jewish Qabalah and had preoccupied the mighty J. S. Bach himself.

On the following Saturday evening we listened to the football results, although I had no idea what they meant. Dad started getting excited but covered it up well and when all the results had been given he checked the coupon again and then again. Cautioning us against false hope he paced around the room until the end of the programme, when the pools dividends were finally announced. Our selection paid out exactly £80.

Shortly after, I was the proud recipient of a brand new Richardson violin built to a Guarnerius model, which meant it was broad and flat with big sexy hips and an 'open', generous carriage. (The language of violins is voluptuous, as befits their inherent femininity.)

Of course she was perfect in my eyes – even when I discovered that she also sported a strange and sticky orange-red varnish and weighed in at a fleshy half a tonne. Richardson was one of those compulsively innovative makers, convinced he could 'improve' on the masters. His violins had far too much wood in them and he had also developed a particularly unfortunate varnish that became so tacky whenever it was hot that my hand would stick to it, leaving permanent imprints.

Nor was his proprietary varnish impervious to salt, and over the years the lower right side of the belly grew streaky and almost bare where I had shed hot, lonely tears on it when practising.

Was this fortuitous win the miracle I felt it was? For those who cannot tolerate or contemplate synchronicity this story must join the pantheon of other statistically unlikely coincidences. Try as I might, I still cannot accept a purely mathematical interpretation, but what is beyond doubt is that this incident occurred in such a way and at such an impressionable age that it undoubtedly shaped and reinforced my world view.

An ideal musical childhood

Psychologists have observed that musically gifted children are often the product of somewhat dysfunctional, non-musician parents who have a high regard for music.

The theory goes something like this. Having dysfunctional parents is likely to drive a precocious child into taking the responsible 'parental' role on themselves and they thus tend to become highly self-motivated. Non-practising music-lovers cannot pressure their children with supposedly 'well-informed' criticism, but will always readily support and praise their offspring's slightest musical achievements, so that the child remains unburdened by self-doubt and negativity. This theory attracts me because I could well be a perfect example of such a scenario.

In our household there was also another very real advantage in dedicating myself to practising as this was the one activity that commanded respect and privacy from my mother, who was otherwise obtrusive in the extreme.

All of this and much more beside gave me a profound reliance on my inner musical world with the violin as its external instrument. As the stresses on my parents increased, the violin became my only entirely reliable source of a continuing connection with the world at large and music was the divine force that ruled both my universe and my personal fate.

A family wedding

Shortly after my dad returned from hospital, a plush envelope arrived enclosing the one and only invitation we ever received to a family event. It was from my mum's sister Stella, inviting us to her daughter's wedding. It was notable in that it included six blank pages headed with the instruction: 'List those family members who you would not on any account be willing to sit next to.'

The seating plan took six months to finalise. It sparked my curiosity, because I'd never met any of these people and had no notion of 'Jewishness'. Mum's vocabulary was sprinkled with Yiddish swear words that I often used myself although I did not know what they meant.

After the lengthy marriage ceremony, conducted in Hebrew, the guests reconvened at a sumptuous hotel in Golders Green and I found myself standing among a crowd of strangers, surrounded on every side by tables laden with exotic food.

Dad had deliberately eaten very little during the previous week. At one point he rushed past carrying some salmon and rye bread. He whispered to me not to eat too much, but

I couldn't heed his advice. I'd never imagined that such wonderful food existed.

Mysteriously, no one else seemed to be eating very much at all, and after about an hour, by which time I was utterly stuffed, a little bell sounded and a voice announced, 'Dinner is served.'

Everyone moved eagerly forward to find their places and the months of planning finally paid off. At each place setting was a menu – describing the fifteen courses that were about to be served.

I had struggled as far as the sixth course when a whole chicken was placed before me with some ceremony. I felt the tears welling up. At home we had chicken only very rarely as a special treat and even then it was one small bird between the three of us. A few places away I could see my dad setting about his task with the determined focus of a marathon runner. He was clearly intent on consuming every available scrap and actually succeeded in doing so, although it left him looking like a skinny python that had swallowed a goat. When we finally got home he could do little but lie immobile on the sofa for three days.

Halfway through the feast, a delicious sorbet was served, followed by an informal interval during which people circulated around the tables exchanging gossip with old friends and long-lost cousins. During this hiatus a handwritten message was delivered to my mother, inviting her to bring me to meet her sister and their close family at the high table.

I saw Mum discussing this intensely with my dad, who was definitely not included in the invitation. He waved his hands at her, spluttering with his mouth full, 'Why not go? What harm can it do?'

Mum seized my hand in her own, which was so tense that it felt like a bony claw, and led me between the tables to where the family zealots were sitting on a raised dais, like fleshy apostles lifted from Leonardo da Vinci's depiction of the Last Supper, surveying the gathered assembly below.

Mum's sister Stella was in pride of place, clearly dominating the whole event. It was first time they had spoken for more than ten years.

'Hello, Esther,' she said, greeting my mother. Until then I never knew my mother was called Esther, she was always called Tessa at home.

'Hello, Stella,' my mother replied sullenly.

After a few awkward pleasantries, Stella looked at me. 'So this must be Paul?' she enquired graciously.

Everyone along the high table turned their heads to stare at me hungrily. (It was only much later that I learned that, according to Jewish custom, I was of an age to become eligible to enter the Jewish community, and could have been embraced once more into the family via the rite of passage of a Bar Mitzvah.)

'And we hear he wants to become a violinist,' Stella continued, to an added stirring of interest along the table.

'Yes,' Mum replied. 'We're keeping our fingers crossed.'

Stella drew a deep breath. 'Oh, please, Esther, you know better than to use language like that in front of the Rabbi.'

The grave and bearded Rabbi looked uncomfortable.

My mum was confused. I could see her trying to work out what she might have said to cause offence. Suddenly the penny dropped. 'Oh, you mean crossed,' she said, and instantly lost her temper. 'So what should I say if I want to cross the road?' she demanded in a shrill voice. 'Or decide to cross something out, or even just wake up feeling cross?' Her voice became ever more furious with each example. The Rabbi was now studiously staring at some far distant place, Jerusalem perhaps, and the residents of the high table were fluttering in outrage and concern. Imagine bringing such upset to this joyous day!

That was my sole foray into the delights of Jewish family life.

Mum was made of tough fibre and was still nagging, washing up and spontaneously dancing well into her nineties. By then the only other surviving member of her family was her sister Stella. Quite by chance we discovered that not only was Stella still alive but had recently come to live only a few miles away. Following my own illness I became convinced that it was vital for my mum and her sister to be reconciled, but Mum would have none of it.

'She knows what she has to do. She only has to apologise,' she insisted stubbornly each time I raised the subject.

Towards the end, Stella's daughter contacted us to ask whether we would be willing to undertake DNA blood tests because Stella's brilliant son was dying of motor neurone disease and he hoped that capturing our family history in this way might help advance medical knowledge regarding this devastating and cruel illness.

It was only then that I discovered that this unknown cousin was an eminent historian, Tony Judt, and that for a short time we had both been members of the same European Cultural Parliament. Sadly, we were destined never to meet.

About four years after my own survival my mum lay dying in the same hospital where I had been treated, angrily demanding that I tell her why she was suffering so much. I made the only answer I could: 'I can tell you what I believe, but I know you wouldn't accept it if I did. You must find your own answers.'

This impossibly difficult conversation was rehearsed in slightly different words each day for weeks. She was so angry that I finally seriously doubted the wisdom of my visiting her at all. But suddenly, on her final day, we found an utterly transformed person waiting for us. She greeted us with a huge smile, brimming with joyful happiness.

'I've got it at last,' she said. 'I finally figured out what this thing called life is all about. It all makes sense!'

She told us that she now realised how foolish she had been regarding her sister, saying with great amusement, 'If she came in now, you know what? She'd say, "Tessa, you're a silly cow" – and she'd be right.'

She insisted that we should try to befriend her sister's relatives and become a family once again. Then she said to me, 'Now, Paul, what you've got to do is go off and have fun . . . just have fun!' Still smiling ecstatically, she shut her eyes.

We all waited, until at last a wise old nurse persuaded us to go home. Sure enough, as soon as we left the hospital they called to say that she had died. True to her nature, Mum was perverse and independent to the very last. Bless her.

Selling my violin

Selling my violin felt as if it obliged me to trust in some benign force or divine providence far greater than myself.

This unexpected consequence of illness confirmed my previous intimations that we are able to adapt to almost any changing conditions and even forgo everything we love, as long as we *elect not to dwell upon it*. So, once the decision was made, I bought a very nice modern violin and played it exclusively while my magnificent fiddle remained in its case, waiting to be sold.

I did not open the case to look at it or even have it in the room with me and, when it was finally sold, made a point of not bidding it goodbye. Why tempt fate or torment myself?

Approached like this, our attachment to objects is a good deal easier to deal with than our attachment to people. Objects do not need us whereas people can need us, or at least believe they do. Worse still, we may even persuade ourselves that *they* need *us*. Being ill is a very powerful way of shedding unnecessary attachments, particularly the deep and abiding need for such things as a career, success and public recognition.

Nonetheless, some aspects of ourselves cling on tenaciously to the very end and these represent our deepest illusions.

Before having been so ill the idea of 'letting go' like this would have seemed impossible, but human beings are amazingly adaptable and can continue to experience a sense of completeness even in straitened circumstances. From this perspective on the world the individual or family can represent the whole universe – as it does for the young child.

The size of the canvas is irrelevant to the quality of the reward; this is borne out constantly in the musical world. Nobody with any understanding would consider that Bach diminished himself when writing the *Chaconne* for a single solo violin or that Beethoven reduced his mastery by composing the late quartets rather than adding to his mighty symphonic output.

To me the only thing that still seems difficult is to trust myself to know how to let go of life itself when the time comes. This is perplexing because actually dying was not at all challenging to me when it happened, but now that the time of my demise grows more imminent it would clearly be much easier if I could truly embrace my own insignificance. Holding onto some absurd fantasy that I am some kind of Mahlerian choral symphonic edifice is surely hubristic – but then so is clinging onto one's family as if they are a little string quartet.

As Viktor Frankl concluded, it is hope for the future that provides us with the will to live and creates meaning in our lives – and as long as life has meaning we cleave to it.

But maybe we also have to learn that our personal future can exist only within our imagination and at the appropriate moment our will to live and sense of meaning are also ultimately imaginary and were never 'ours' to lay claim to.

Our culture currently denigrates the world of imagination as somehow being untrue or unreliable. As it is if we choose to measure reality only in terms of facts. But then, as Samuel Arbesman and others have demonstrated, the 'half-life of scientific facts' currently runs at anything between five and forty-five years, the time that typically elapses between a particular set of scientific 'truths' remaining 'true' and their being superseded and becoming obsolete.

This is why human beings remain so drawn to philosophy and religion, and might also account for the extraordinary potency of certain inner musical truths, such as those discernible within the music of Bach, Beethoven, Mozart and Schubert.

No one can be completely sure of 'knowing' the truth but we can most certainly establish a surprisingly durable internal sense or 'taste' for truthfulness in our strivings towards integrated interpretations of our-Selves.

I fail to gain entry to the Menuhin School

That I first discovered my love for the violin when I was eight years old was considered rather late in the accepted scale of such things, for most gifted string players begin their studies at a much earlier age.

By the age of eleven I had already made great strides under the tutelage of my local violin teacher, Mr Gilette-Smith.

I never knew his Christian name; he was known to everyone simply as 'Gilly'. My progress had been so rapid that, with Gilly's approval, and despite having no money to pay the extravagant fees, my parents encouraged me to audition for a place at Yehudi Menuhin's newly opened school for gifted young musicians on the unlikely chance that I might gain a scholarship.

The interview was not a success. Although Menuhin was undoubtedly a wonderfully sensitive man and a true maestro, we were separated by an unbridgeable social and cultural gulf which made any understanding between us quite impossible.

When I arrived at the school, Menuhin's assistant, Robert Masters, was already there, as was a middle-aged lady, who was casually introduced to me as the 'accompanist'.

This was confusing. I had no idea what an accompanist was, or why she was there at all, but before there was any chance of elucidation the atmosphere changed and the great man entered. Like Gilly, he was very small and not at all frightening or overpowering, although he certainly had a commanding presence. He made a point of speaking kindly to me and asked me to play my prepared piece, the first movement of Beethoven's 'Spring' Sonata.

Embarking on my performance I was considerably distracted by the pianist, who suddenly and quite inexplicably simultaneously began clattering busily away on her keyboard. I was far too shy to comment about this although it was a total surprise and terribly difficult to ignore.

Incredible though it might seem, no one had ever thought to tell me that this violin sonata had a *piano* part – still less that it had quite naturally been arranged for me to perform it with a pianist. I recall Menuhin making disturbed rumbling noises as I played and then when I had finished asking me a number of questions about the music, none of which I could answer or even understand – after which I left.

Although he was refusing me a place, he took the trouble to write my parents a kindly personal letter in which he remarked that although I showed great talent, he was surprised by how little I seemed to understand the music I played. In any case, he said, there was then simply no funding for a scholarship. I realise now that Menuhin's privileged early life must have made it entirely incomprehensible to him that any gifted young violinist would not know that a Beethoven violin sonata was a duet with piano.

My parents were clearly rendered distraught by this letter but I noticed that both they and Gilly were tremendously careful to try to shelter me from the disappointment. On the evening after the letter arrived I heard raised, anxious voices and discovered Gilly with my parents, obviously attempting to placate them. When they realised I was listening an intense silence fell.

Dad finally took the plunge and began telling me that I hadn't succeeded, but not to be too depressed. Immediately Gilly chipped in to say that he thought this was most probably all for the best as he was now going to prepare me to approach his own violin hero, the fine Armenian violinist, Manoug Parikian.

Although I did feel some sense of failure it didn't really break my heart. Menuhin was clearly a kind man but I had felt completely out of my depth with him and his circle – who had all seemed to me to belong to an entirely alien, godlike species.

I am sent to boarding school

If we always insist on a rational understanding of the world, we spend much of our time explaining away life's richness, but once we accept an existence shaped by a divinity we can then risk reshaping our common sense in order to support that thesis instead.

My lengthy run-in with mortality has certainly tipped me heavily in favour of this second option and I now find myself struggling to find reasons *not* to believe in a conscious design-er, aka God. In this new reality my life now seems to have been, and continues to be, particularly richly endowed with meaningful episodes.

Shortly after the farrago of my failing entry into the Menu-hin School, my mother also fell ill. With both of them now struggling and sick, my parents became deeply anxious about what would become of me should they both die. It was clear that no one else in their extended family would wish to take me in.

Gilly persuaded them to let me take up a scholarship at a boarding school where he taught. Although his intention was clearly generous, the school turned out to be the kind of third-rate public school that had originally catered for the sons of vicars and impecunious army officers. By the time I got there it had lost even those pretensions and many of the boys were from broken homes or were illegitimate and unwanted. It was a rough and ugly establishment, rife with bullying and bug-gery. I hated everything about it.

Since I was the sole musical star of the school's end-of-year showcases, I was granted a few privileges, such as a classroom to practise in after school hours and, at my dad's insistence, exemption from the Combined Cadet Force or 'Scouts'. This enlightened attempt completely backfired. From then on I was naturally perceived as the school sissy and bullied unmerciful-ly. As ever when unhappy, I retreated into my violin playing.

I déjà vu a concerto

CLYTEMNESTRA Can you not hear the music?
ELEKTRA It comes from myself.

Hugo von Hofmannsthal's libretto for Richard Strauss's *Elektra*

One evening I was practising in a lonely classroom far away from the rest of the children, terrified as usual by surround-ing darkness and loneliness. The school was in a remote cor-ner of the Cotswold hills, there was no outside lighting, and I was facing my usual dilemma of whether to return through the blackness to the bullying crowd or remain a bit longer in frightened isolation.

As I played, quite without warning I found myself transported to a completely different environment. Instead of the featureless classroom, I was standing before an orchestra dressed in old-fashioned concert garb, a particularly stiff form of evening wear, and playing from memory a concerto that in my ordinary twentieth-century consciousness I had no knowledge of whatever.

This rich 'memory' went on for some time and I recall seeing before me a theatre or concert hall with an upper balcony at the rear and sides. I was also very aware of the front-rank orchestral string players sitting near me, and of the conductor on his podium. As I was experiencing all this I could feel that my chest was that of a fully grown man and that I was at last playing with a wonderfully quick and expressive vibrato. At thirteen, my vibrato was floppy and slow and remained so for many years. This vision, or memory, slowly faded and to my intense desolation I found myself once again a little boy playing in a cold impersonal classroom.

I rushed back to the school house and sought out the housemaster whose fussy, dull Christianity I felt might provide a degree of insight. Instead, he looked nonplussed and sent me to the sanatorium where a matron told me that a good night's sleep would probably put paid to such wild imaginings. So much for sharing the intimations of another lifetime. Apart from the power of the incident itself, I learned not to confide such intimate matters to other people.

According to my calculations, at about this age I would have fulfilled the five thousand hours of practice nowadays quoted as the necessary criterion to achieve instrumental competence. I am not suggesting that my powerful musical déjà vu was necessarily associated with this milestone but I do wonder whether my 'inner self' gave its consent for me to receive this affirming boost.

Such episodes could easily be the product of an imaginative young mind but I remain particularly impressed that it brought me direct knowledge of what a grown man's chest and arms felt like ten or fifteen years before I had developed them. For that reason, even though many people would relegate this experience to the box marked 'over-imaginative', I must include it as a powerful supportive event in my own musical development.

Manoug Parikian becomes my teacher

Fortunately, despite his naivety with regard to the school, Gilly was as good as his word about trying to set me up with Manoug Parikian as a teacher.

Manoug did not usually teach youngsters and before even considering taking me on as a pupil he insisted I undertake a formal interview. He began by asking me whether I wanted to become an amateur or a professional player. I was offended by this question and my face obviously reflected my dismay. Seeing this, he turned to Gilly, who was listening nervously.

'You see I teach all sorts, amateurs and professionals, and although I'm happy to teach either I make it quite clear before we start because they get a different kind of lesson.'

Clearly overawed as ever, poor Gilly was rendered inarticulate. 'Aaaargh,' he gurgled appreciatively.

Much as Manoug loved receiving Gilly's adoration, he was

also a little embarrassed by it, hence his rather awkward con-descension.

Looking at me with apparent detachment he pursued his enquiry. 'So which do you want to be?'

'A professional, of course,' I replied.

Manoug looked suitably grave and turned again to Gilly. 'You see, if someone wants to become a professional I have rules.' Then to me: 'You understand that I demand total obedience?' I nodded. 'I expect you to do regular practice every day without exception, and I will not tolerate anyone missing lessons for any reason whatever.'

He turned to Gilly again. 'Leopold Auer says that everybody needs to do a minimum of three hours a day or four, if they're slow. Get him to buy the Carl Flesch scale book, we'll start with that, and only that, for the first year, after which we can add etudes!' He went on, 'How old were you when you started?'

'Eight,' I replied.

He looked genuinely concerned at this. 'So we've already got four years to make up – you are going to have to practise for four hours every day. Do you understand?'

Gilly seemed daunted by this, but I was elated. At last I was really going to get going. It seemed entirely self-evident to me that only dedicated hard work was going to make me perfect.

Practising

At twelve years old, four hours of daily practice seems an inordinately long time, particularly when you have only scales and arpeggios to play, but I gradually learned to depend on the exhaustion and tedium. I also discovered that after about three or four hours of good work I would reach a 'golden' patch when my playing would suddenly become free and 'easy'. This provided a daily taste of the kind of perfection that sports psychologists might now describe as 'flow' and it made all the hard work worthwhile. I also discovered that if I watched myself in the mirror and attended closely to my breathing as I practised, I could reach a serene, detached state. This also had the useful effect of arresting coughs and colds, which I noticed spontaneously retreated from such 'treatment'.

I don't know why I became so interested in the relationship between breath control and gesture, which to the best of my knowledge is not something that has ever been taught in the violin world, but it became clear to me that this was the only way I could establish total physical and emotional control.

In this way, over those years, I somehow formulated a personal 'yoga' of violin playing. Part of the magic of such controlled breathing was an ability to let go of any unhelpful mental commentary while still acting with intent and attention.

In our culture it is generally considered quite normal to *stop* breathing while undertaking complex tasks, but truly talented individuals never do this. Top-class golfers, snooker players and others are, if anything, even more relaxed at critical moments of their game, and the same is true of all great instrumentalists. Such lightness and sureness of touch is always a sign of the type of enhanced competence we call 'greatness'.

A medical friend specialising in musicians' repetitive strain injuries has established that when attempting to sight-read very difficult music, amateur pianists apply significantly increased levels of finger pressure. Conversely, gifted professional players universally lighten their finger pressure in response to the increased technical demands of sight-reading challenging new scores.

'Tartini tones'

Music and the rich world of the violin is full of subtle analogies and invitations to philosophical reflection. For example, 'double-stopping', which on the violin involves simultaneously playing two notes at the same time, will evoke a third 'ghost' pitch created by their resultant frequencies. This natural phenomenon is known as 'Tartini tones', after the eighteenth-century violin master Giuseppe Tartini, who is still credited with their discovery, although he was certainly not the first to describe them.

Traditionally schooled violinists, such as I became when studying with Manoug, learn to check the accuracy of their tuning when double-stopping by listening to these 'ghost' tones, which provide the performer with an alternative musical narrative unheard by the audience.

After a while this strange, slightly eerie intoning becomes a constant commentary on the truth or accuracy of what we are playing, rather along the lines of an awakened conscience, or the invisible psychic aura that many mystics claim surrounds us all – and which science is now beginning to confirm. What then is the music we really play? The notes we all hear, or the evoked combination of them all, or some other narrative altogether?

Manoug was very conservative in his approach to violin teaching and all these traditional protocols had to be followed in every particular. No one knows just how far back some of these methods date, but it is clear to me that a great deal of ancient philosophy and esoteric knowledge has been carried across the ages by the study of musical laws. This method must have been particularly potent in the era before written notation or books existed, since, with its combination of gesture and sound, musical memory establishes profound neural networks of recall.

I leave my ghastly boarding school

After I had suffered three miserable years of abandonment in this horrible school, my parents finally picked up on my deep unhappiness and even began to show some concern about the widespread livid bruising on my arms, the result of being constantly beaten up.

By great good fortune by this time things had also changed for the better at home. Despite his constant pain and continuing heart problems, Dad was doing pretty well in his business. Mum had also successfully survived a fairly serious gynaecological operation and, to top it all, against all the odds we won the football pools again – but this time our winnings were substantial.

On the proceeds of this second win we were able to move into a far nicer house and keep the original one in the Cowley Road for the business. Dad and Mum were even able to purchase another house as an investment property.

By now I was about fourteen years old. Despite my natural intelligence I had lost any interest I might have had in academic attainment. We discovered that I needed only five O levels in order to qualify for a student grant. I enrolled at the local technical college to study for these exams.

The main advantage of the technical college was that I could practise all day long without anyone bothering about what I was up to. By then all I was interested in was continuing my studies with Manoug at the Royal Academy of Music (the RAM) where he was a professor.

In the meantime Dad continued to pay for me to have weekly private lessons as he had throughout the hard times.

Manoug taught me at his home a few miles outside Oxford. Despite his affectations of grandeur, I was never very impressed by his apparent lack of interest in me and my parents. From remarks he occasionally let drop, I think he assumed that I was some kind of spoilt rich kid with a well-to-do father who thought nothing of paying out inflated sums of money for his little boy to learn the violin. How little he knew. And how easily he could – and should – have sought to understand our situation better.

But, as I was gradually to discover for myself, Manoug had identity problems of his own.

Becoming English

Manoug had been born in Turkey in 1920 and brought up in Cyprus. In common with so many immigrants, and in marked contrast to his instrumental poise, he was painfully insecure about his place in English society. Insecure myself, I became fascinated and amused by his attempts to conform and become 'English'. I'm sure he would have greatly appreciated his current Wikipedia entry, which describes him as 'a British concert violinist'.

When we first met, he was living with his family in a lovely old vicarage in Oxfordshire, where he had surrounded himself with every accoutrement of 'English-ness', including fine paintings, a beautiful garden, a gracious and lovely English wife and so on. Yet, even with his perfectly modulated 'Oxford' accent and impressive vocabulary, Manoug remained somehow irredeemably foreign.

In later years I came to understand that his childhood was lived in the shadow of the Armenian genocide that took place in Turkey and the Ottoman Empire between 1915 and 1924 when up to 1.5 million died. Ethnic Armenians fled to other countries if they possibly could.

Despite my mother coming from a large family of poverty-stricken Russian-Romanian Jewish immigrants and my father being a dispossessed Geordie and a political outcast, it never crossed my mind that anyone might feel the need to be accepted as part of something as abstract as 'society'. Occupied in constructing my own identity at the time, I had no idea that such a thing existed.

Each week I would arrive promptly for my hour's lesson and almost every week would observe, with bemusement, Manoug adopting some new affectation in his pursuit of an elusive 'Englishness'.

A portrait of Manoug

One memorable day, as I arrived at his house, Manoug came strutting out, every inch Toad of Toad Hall, decked out in plus fours and a shooting jacket, all brand new and purchased without regard for expense. With studied nonchalance he was carrying an expensive shotgun over one arm. When I enquired about this impressive new acquisition, he remarked airily that he had decided to deal with the 'squirrel problem'.

The following week he was noticeably less avuncular and although the weather was glorious I found him seated in his customary place in the teaching room. Noticing the gun was now languishing neglected in the corner of the room, at the end of the lesson I asked him about his shooting exploits. Looking distinctly uncomfortable, he muttered something about not really doing it any more as 'no one could possibly shoot squirrels because they move so fast'.

Later I discovered that Manoug's enormous liquid brown eyes were extremely short-sighted. My guess is that he had considerable difficulty even spotting a squirrel let alone aiming at one.

Another week he took up smoking. I saw at once that something was up when I spotted an elegant onyx cigarette lighter and a silver cigarette case placed strategically on his handsome, leather-topped, period writing desk.

Sure enough, at just the right moment in the lesson – not too near the beginning, so that I would appreciate this was a natural action rather than a piece of theatre choreographed for my benefit, yet early enough to ensure that there was enough time to play out the whole ceremony within the duration of the lesson – Manoug set about casually lighting a cigarette. We both knew that this was a performance but the unspoken rules obliged us to play out the tacit ritual with insouciance.

As I trudged through my obligatory Kreutzer study, Manoug opened the newly acquired cigarette case and with graceful affectation lifted out a slim black cigarette. He passed this slowly beneath his enormous nostrils and a look of deep satisfaction suffused his handsome olive face. His eyes were still half shut, and the exquisite cigarette lighter was lifted from its place of honour on the desktop and, with the cigarette now placed between his lips, he leant forward and flicked the lighter.

No flame appeared. He flicked again with no result and an affronted wrinkle marred the smooth vastness of his nose. This was not at all how he'd rehearsed it. After several more futile efforts he finally picked up the offending lighter and, glancing up to make sure I wasn't observing his embarrassment, rattled it vigorously until it grudgingly lit up. Having got the cigarette to light he settled down but then interrupted my playing, saying, 'No, that's not really how this needs to be played. Listen . . .'

Picking up his priceless Stradivarius from the piano lid, he began to demonstrate his point. Between his lips the cigarette was still burning and it soon began to spill hot ash onto the exquisite seventeenth-century instrument. Seeing my concern, he stopped for a moment and, although knowing the answer full well, asked what was worrying me. I told him and he explained that there was no risk to the varnished surface as the ash cooled so quickly.

He also went out of his way to tell me that these were no ordinary cigarettes but rare and expensive Balkan Sobranies imported direct from Russia. This failed to impress me as I'd seen my father nearly die from a heart attack and consequently give up smoking. To prove his point he proceeded to play the entire study from memory with the cigarette smouldering between his lips. As he played, the smoke began to curl up into a lethal column inexorably winding upwards into one of his huge nostrils.

Manoug's eyes began to water as he desperately fought against a choking cough. As ever, he seemed completely incapable of recognising when to admit defeat. He played on in increasing agony, one eye almost closed in pain as the poisonous smoke filled his hapless sinuses. By the end he couldn't speak and vaguely waved an arm to indicate that I should play the study once more, which I duly did. Behind me I could hear him attempting to suppress a fit of retching.

When autumn arrived, Manoug decided that his elegant Georgian living room would benefit from an open fire burning in the marble fireplace. In order to complete the effect he had bought himself a fine set of brass fire-irons and a magnificent pair of antique bellows, all leather and brass.

Having given me a brief analytical history of bellows in general, it was clear that this lesson was going to be punctuated by regular ritual visitations to aerate the log fire, which was already burning brightly.

I duly began performing my weekly cycle of scales and arpeggios. Sure enough, after a few minutes Manoug rose from his chair and stepped fastidiously across the room to play with his new toy. He leant down and inserted the nozzle of the bellows into the base of the burning logs and began puffing away. It worked perfectly.

With tangible relief Manoug stood up, far too quickly, and with a sickening thump struck his head directly against the solid marble mantelpiece. He reeled and almost fell over. I readied myself to leap forward and save him from falling into the fire, but he rallied, so I kept on going.

He tottered to his chair and slumped over the desk. After a while he recovered sufficiently to ask me rather curtly to play another set of scales. I was doing this when with horrified disbelief I saw him again get up from his chair and make his way to the fireplace. Once more he went through the ritual of the bellows and then in what seemed to me like slow motion he again rose directly beneath the slab of unforgiving rock awaiting him.

This time it was much worse. I actually saw the top of his fleshy, bald head spread like an over-ripe melon as it struck the underside of the mantelpiece. An involuntary groan escaped his lips, his knees buckled and it was only by good fortune that he fell away from the waiting flames and managed to reach the safe haven of his chair unaided. In evident agony he sat unmoving, cradling his head in his hands for the rest of the lesson and managed only an incoherent grunt when it came time for me to leave.

Towards the end of the time while I was having lessons with Manoug at his home, he bought a huge and unpleasant Alsatian dog, who found me irresistible. I loathed and feared this slobbering hound and its amorous attentions.

Despite all his little foibles and vanities, Manoug was a scrupulous teacher. He also had a certain covert warmth, although he went to immense lengths to hide it.

Manoug's winning side

Occasionally, quite without warning, Manoug would reveal another, warmer and more passionate side to his character. I once heard him wax lyrical about the way that the supreme twentieth-century master of the violin, Jascha Heifetz, played the opening scale of Saint-Saëns's *Havanaise*, which he described as 'a kind of perfection – an example of the ultimate in violin playing'. He was right, of course, but only a true connoisseur would recognise the supreme genius within such an apparently insignificant fragment.

One day he noticed that the frog (the tightening mechanism) at the end of my bow was not working properly because the little screw had lost its thread. He warned me against taking it to anyone but a true craftsman to mend and told me this story. 'One day the bell on my precious bicycle broke. I was just a child and thought it would be wonderful to have a brand new bell, so I took it to the village cobbler, who also used to mend bicycles, thinking that he would fit a nice new one. But to my disappointment he didn't even think to sell me a new bell. Instead he took the rusty old one off the bike and opened it up on his bench. He then took out the spring and showed me how it was broken. Taking a sheet of metal he carefully used his clasp knife to cut a long strip off one side of it. He rolled the thin strip around his pencil to form it into a spring and then fitted it back into the bell where it worked perfectly for years.'

As he reminisced his face was lit up with charming softness and appreciation and, clearly much moved by his memories, he carried on quietly as if to himself. 'You see that's the kind of craftsmanship that really matters, when someone truly cares and has a knowledge of what they're doing and takes real pride and pleasure in doing their craft well. That's so rare nowadays . . .'

At this level of instinctive emotional intelligence and

appreciation Manoug was a real thoroughbred, with a genuine respect for other naturally gifted players – and so, inevitably for him as with most others of his generation, the flawless Heifetz was God.

I always felt that Manoug would have made a wonderful quartet leader, but this was not an aspiration that he ever shared or at least chose to acknowledge.

I become a student at the Royal Academy of Music

I duly passed the required five O levels at the local technical college – one at least by dint of some judicious cheating – and received a scholarship place at the Royal Academy of Music, although I shouldn't have as I was only fifteen. When they discovered this the Academy authorities attempted to block my attendance but at the same time Dad received a letter from the local council to tell him that I was not eligible for a means-tested grant because his income was too large.

When I was called into the registrar's office about this I was therefore fortunately able to point out that the Academy did not risk losing its tuition fees (which was clearly the main concern), and asked whether the RAM really wanted to lose me as a student over such a minor technicality.

I never heard another word about it. But this small happenstance established an oddly stroppy strand in my attitude towards the Academy and I was to have many similar run-ins with RAM officialdom during my stay there.

I quickly discovered that the Academy authorities took a very different approach towards those students who were likely to become 'starry' performers from how it handled all the others. As I never assumed anything less than 'stardom' for myself I indulged myself outrageously.

I foolishly refused to attend harmony and counterpoint classes or anything else other than my personal lessons with Manoug and the weekly rehearsals of the first orchestra, which was the Academy's prestige showcase and which I was therefore naturally aspiring to lead.

At the end of my first year, however, I suffered something of a reality check regarding the orchestra's glitzy conductor, who was a gifted professional and the assistant conductor to the wonderful Sir John Barbirolli and the Hallé Orchestra.

Observing my obvious admiration of this flamboyant 'carver', my desk mate in the violin section discreetly confided that she was this conductor's girlfriend and that they would shortly be moving to Canada together. She went on to tell me to take note of how in performance this showy character had a silk bandana saturated with menthol tucked into his top pocket to deploy at moments of high musical emotion, so that he could display to the audience his noble suffering profile as he wept 'real' tears.

I checked this out – and was so appalled by its truth that when he duly offered me the leader's chair for the following year I immediately refused his blandishments point blank.

This led to my immediate summons to the registrar's office, where this conductor first sought to negotiate, then pleaded with me to lead for him. But I was implacable. Overtaken by impotent fury, he began shouting dire threats about how he would 'destroy my career', screaming finally, 'And if that happens who'll be laughing then, eh?'

At this critical juncture something really naughty possessed me and I found myself saying, 'Well, you may be right, but just at the moment I must say I'm really enjoying myself!' As I was saying this I happened to catch the registrar's eye and saw that he was bent double, desperately trying not to laugh.

I also refused to take any examinations, and for some months even took to arriving ostentatiously attired in my pyjamas. Was this some kind of inarticulate expression of anger towards this conductor? I wonder.

In short, I must have been a complete pain in the bum – but everyone seemed to put up with it, presumably because my passion for the violin was so tangible, or maybe it was just that they'd seen it all before.

Given my immature isolated intensity and prevailing sense of emotionally insecure superiority, this was perhaps all inevitable. The best that can be said of it was that it was, in its own incoherent way, at least principled and sincere. The shame of it is that it has taken me until now to begin to see it for the confused adolescent posturing it was.

Another factor in my burgeoning arrogance was the distorted influence of arguably the greatest violinist of them all: the masterly Jascha Heifetz. Now that this magician of the violin is an increasingly remote figure for aspiring violinists, we are beginning to lose sight of just how commanding a player he was for much of the twentieth century.

Heifetz and the pursuit of perfection

'There are many violinists — then there is Heifetz . . .'

David Oistrakh

'If you provoke a jealous God by playing with such super-human perfection you will die young. I earnestly advise you to play something badly every night before going to bed, instead of saying your prayers. No mortal should presume to play so faultlessly.' A personal letter from Bernard Shaw to the nineteen-year-old Jascha Heifetz following his Carnegie Hall debut concert

In 1969, when I first entered the Royal Academy of Music on a violin scholarship, the only mandatory event was to attend a viewing of two short films showing Heifetz in performance. The whole violin faculty was there, including all the violin professors. Despite being rather dated and 'cheesy', these films beautifully illustrate the great player in his full majesty.

During one of Heifetz's most impressive pyrotechnical displays, one of the professors who had played a concerto himself just the week before at the Proms remarked jokingly, 'We might as well all give up!' The remark brought a dispir-ited murmur of acquiescence from his fellow teachers. One sequence in particular made an immense impression on me. Filmed in slow motion, the master was playing runs in thirds, all in down-bow staccato, which is one of the most dazzling technical feats the instrument can demand.

Heifetz was clearly simultaneously listening to what he was playing and responding to what he heard by constantly adjust-ing the positions of his left-hand fingers as they moved across the strings. This observation was so surprising because the most striking features of Heifetz's playing were his diamond-pure articulation and almost percussive precision. Indeed, generations of aspiring young players destroyed themselves attempting to emulate this distinctive style by over-playing and generally striving too hard.

But, unlike his imitators, Heifetz himself was subtle and gentle in his approach to the instrument and, most significantly, clearly remained proactive and extraordinarily alert in his response to the constant uncertainties of performance.

Attention in performance

It was clear that Heifetz had established such a unique integration of mind and emotion that his performance was simultaneously controlled and spontaneous. There was no denying his uniqueness or his fabulous virtuosity – but how could this paradox be understood, still less imitated?

Part of the answer seems to lie in the sheer level of unbroken and highly focused attention he gave to what he was doing. Watching him play was rather like spying on a panther – all stealth, poise and pent-up energy. He never wasted any effort on extraneous gestures nor set out merely to please or ingratiate himself with his audience and so his expenditure of energy appeared to be minimal. Once he was weighed before and after playing a concerto and was found to have lost in the order of six pounds. What looked like spending the minimal amount of energy was clearly generating an extraordinary musical intensity.

Heifetz and imperfection

The myths that surround Heifetz's playing – his technical mastery, his demanding nature and commanding presence – have combined to produce the impression of an austere and impenetrable persona. It is interesting to note that, wonderful performer though he was, he seems, as a teacher, to have often had a destructive influence.

Having studied films of his masterclasses I conclude that although he was perhaps not an inspired teacher he was not a bad one either. In my view, all he did was tell the unvarnished truth, only to be misunderstood by his worshipping pupils – as is so often the fate of spiritual gurus.

He was at his most devastating when he performed pieces to demonstrate to his students how they could sound. His musical personality was so dominant and dazzling that as often as not his rendition simply overwhelmed the pupils' own vision, no matter how sincerely arrived at.

Heifetz's dilemma is similar to that of many other forceful personalities. He was constantly probing people in order to discover whether he could dominate them, but only, I like to think, in the hope of finding an equal. It can be terribly dull to be surrounded by acquiescent docility but sadly it can also be addictive. I suspect Heifetz, in common with many other stars and quite a few leaders, had mastered the art of unconsciously undermining those around him.

Many people look for someone to lead them and happily surrender their own critical faculties in order to find such support – but very few ever stop to think of the loneliness their leader is enduring as the price of their quiescence.

Although not for one moment suggesting that I was ever in the same class as Heifetz, I cannot help feeling that I also apparently had a similarly 'crushing' effect on those around me. This at least is what my family and colleagues have often told me.

'Letting go'

One day Manoug announced it was time for me to learn *spiccato*, a technique in which the bow rapidly lifts on-and-off the string in a coordinated fashion like a bouncing ball. It is notoriously difficult to teach and Manoug began by telling me that the essential thing about *spiccato* was 'You can either do it or you can't!'

He gave me some key pointers, including the notion that *spiccato* is not something that can just be 'done' but must be discovered by exploring the bow's innate instability on the string. I quickly discovered that there is just one combination of position, speed and weight when the bow spontaneously begins to bounce on its own. As long as I avoided any attempt to interfere with this motion, the bow would suddenly spring to life, creating a cascade of beautifully light and articulate notes. Once I had discovered this elusive trick it took only a few modifications to be able to play *spiccato* at any speed I chose.

When I returned the following week to show Manoug my new-found trick he listened for just a few moments and then rather curtly cut me off. 'Well, it's just as I said. It's one of those things you can either do or you can't . . . and you obviously can!'

Only after I had the chance to observe Manoug in performance did I understand that despite all his fine qualities this was one of the few gifts he did not really have himself.

Caution versus spontaneity

On one occasion Manoug rather cruelly parodied my careful playing by miming someone trying to ice-skate without letting go of the barrier at the side of the rink. I understood his facetiousness well enough and even agreed with him to a certain extent, but felt I was playing a much longer game than he gave me the credit for. Ironically, Manoug was actually one of the most cautious performers I ever heard and it was one of the features I liked best about his fastidious playing.

The tension between freedom and control is continually being held in balance by any serious performing musician. At every stage we push to the limit and, each time we do, this 'limit' simply becomes a new point of departure, which of course is exactly what creativity demands of us.

I wasn't looking for Manoug to provide this level of musical experience for me. I never felt he had a sufficiently profound emotional or intellectual insight into music to understand it in the terms I demanded.

What I was seeking from him was a sound technique with which to plumb the great chasm beneath my feet. At that stage I had no idea what form this musical search might take and discovered it only later when I committed to becoming a quartet player.

Like so many teenagers, I was deeply critical and judgemental. My view now is that Manoug was a highly gifted and intuitive player with a truly refined sensibility towards the sound and subtle 'stuff' of music. Much of his stature as a player probably derived from deep down within his essentially naive, childlike or innocent 'ear' – which is not at all simple but rather a direct conduit to the universal mind.

We might instinctively recognise that this has much in common with the divine quality that we also discern in birdsong.

Manoug and I part company

Manoug Parikian was an autocratic, old-fashioned pedagogue with a fine career and a polished, aristocratic style of playing. For many years I willingly accepted his authority and did my best to fulfil his many demands.

He continued to be my professor when I took up my scholarship at the Royal Academy but as I matured and formed my own string quartet, the relationship with him faltered. He dismissed my determination to pursue a career as a chamber musician, which I felt I had every right to choose, insisting I follow his own path by aiming to compete successfully at an international violin competition and then go on to become an orchestral leader and occasional concerto player.

We argued and finally parted acrimoniously. Subsequent events revealed that the ties between us were closer than we knew.

While this drama was being played out, I received one excellent lesson from my quartet coach, Sidney Griller, during which he commented that whereas good amateurs will typically practise until they get something right, top professionals must prepare until they *cannot* get it wrong.

It was my observation that Heifetz had gone a significant step beyond even this since he was playing in the certain knowledge that even he was necessarily always going to be 'imperfect'.

So focused and acute was his level of attention and so cat-like were his reactions that he seemed to be able to create more time in the present moment than his fellows could ever hope to possess, a characteristic, as I was to discover, of all those whose exceptional gifts mark them out.

From this I began to develop an understanding that artistic freedom, technical excellence and depth of expression are all the product of expanded attention.

Incidentally an exactly similar, infinite expansion of the present moment can be evident while dying – hence the possibility of a complete 'life review' taking place even within the final few heartbeats of a passing life.

Bruch's Scottish Fantasy

All this is beautifully illustrated in an illuminating film of Heifetz, recorded live in Paris in 1970 when the master was nearly seventy years old, performing one of his greatest showcase works, the *Scottish Fantasy* by Max Bruch. Composed in 1880, this work is really more of a virtuoso vehicle based on a series of folk songs than it is a conventional concerto. The piece is not now considered in any way a masterpiece except perhaps when Heifetz is playing it. The film shows him backstage, preparing to make his entry. As ever, he is perfectly balanced and composed, and most definitely already performing.

He pretends with artless guile not to know how French players wish each other good luck. 'What do they say in this country?' he asks politely.

Someone duly responds with 'Merde.'

'Ah yes, merde, of *course*!' This feigned ignorance from a man who has performed for forty years at every international venue.

We then see him sweeping through the French National Orchestra and onto the front of the stage. As he does so, the audience rises to give him a standing ovation, not for his performance, which is yet to come, but just for being there. This is stardom indeed.

Looking absolutely poised, he takes an age carefully tuning his supreme Stradivarius and proceeds with equally fastidious care to check the tension of his bow. This painstaking ceremony complete, he finally lifts the violin majestically to his chin and prepares to play. Around him the orchestra anxiously mimics him. But just as they are all ready to play the opening chords, Heifetz suddenly lowers his violin, gesturing to the front-desk players that he needs more room. Now he is chivvying them to move back, which involves the whole orchestra shifting their chairs and music stands.

Once again the process of bringing the large ensemble to a state of readiness begins, but by this time the musicians are clearly uncomfortable and only our hero is unaffected and completely in control. At last, Heifetz very slightly shrugs his shoulders and an obviously nervous orchestra raggedly strikes up the opening chord.

It is only now that an alert musician watching this unfolding drama might realise that there is something very amiss with this orchestra. Their corporate performance nerves are also due to the fact that they are missing a vital component – a conductor. Heifetz has decided that his own charisma is quite sufficient to meet the ensemble demands.

I should make it clear that I am no admirer of conductors, quite the contrary, and have spent my life avoiding the whole damned lot of them. But even I recognise that richly scored nineteenth-century Romantic music in the grand tradition such as the Bruch requires serious coordination, and it really must have a competent conductor.

With or without a conductor, a large body of musicians such as this orchestra must at least be given clear directions by someone, either the soloist or the leader or both. Merely shrugging, as Heifetz chooses to do, is to court disaster. Flexing one's charisma may be impressive, but it simply cannot serve as a substitute for the clarity of an unambiguous beat.

Unsurprisingly, this highly competent professional orchestra sounds strained and hesitant in the opening chords, but even after it has somewhat regained its composure it is difficult to grasp the intention or usefulness of the malignant sideways glances that the maestro frequently appears to direct at the cowed viola section.

Heifetz's saving grace, and it is awesome, is that he never fails to meet his own supremely demanding standards. As the orchestra wobbles around him, he enters with flawless stillness and poetic poise, each gesture honed, polished and superbly deliberate.

In later years I always found it possible to overcome my own performance anxiety as soon as I discerned the same terror in my colleagues. Did I unconsciously undermine those around me all that time, and if so was my motivation secretly dictatorial or a form of enlightened responsibility?

That it was probably both is another paradox.

One insight I gained from this remarkable piece of film is that nothing makes you look better than reducing those around you to apparent incompetence, but it is a dangerous strategy that should be risked only when one is confident of being able to deliver a flawless performance oneself.

Kipling called it 'the Law of the Jungle' and it is fine as far as it goes. If you do it well enough it can make you top dog of a husky pack or the leader of an orchestra.

Mere leadership does not make a team and I had to learn that none of this is quite enough to lead a string quartet. So by the time I saw this film I was beginning to suspect that, as was once said of him, 'Heifetz is the greatest player in the world – of second-rate repertoire.'

Heifetz plays a wrong note

A friend was playing in the orchestra when Heifetz made his acclaimed and now historic recording of the *Scottish Fantasy* in the less than salubrious Watford Town Hall. There were to be no ensemble problems on this occasion for Sir Malcolm Sargent was on the podium. Heifetz was already in full, incomparable flow when something unthinkable occurred. Without warning he went wrong and stopped playing.

It's hard to express how utterly incredible this was. This was a man whose infallibility was a legend. Superman falling dead from the skies would have been no greater shock. The whole orchestra stopped in its tracks, the string players particularly dazed by this cataclysmic event.

My friend, a first violinist in the orchestra and sitting almost alongside Heifetz as he played, told me that so magnetic was Heifetz's performance that no one in the orchestra had even been looking at the conductor. When he stopped a stunned silence immediately followed. What would he do? Could he recover? How was everyone expected to behave?

After a moment's ghastly silence, Heifetz, expressionless and impassive as ever, slowly brought his instrument down to the side of his body. Without a word or a single flicker of emotion he turned and walked slowly to one side of the hall where he stood facing the wall. After a long moment he brought his violin back to the playing position and began *practising slow scales*. The orchestral players together with the conductor remained frozen in disbelief, many with their instruments still to their lips or on their shoulders.

After about ten minutes of lonely violin scales the master stalked back to his recording position, gave Sir Malcolm a curt nod and the concerto began again. The resulting performance is one of the miracles of recording history.

Once again I detect that Heifetz's mastery extended to an unusual honesty and poise with regard to his own limitations. This is not to suggest he was in any way tolerant of incompetence – no one who heard him play or met him ever remotely felt this – but as a performer, Heifetz seems to have had an almost unique capacity for self-critical attention combined with a pragmatic sense that events must be managed moment by moment *without any unnecessary negative emotion*.

Even when quite young I realised that while Heifetz was universally adulated, he was not much loved. Inevitably, I wanted both. Never having had siblings, I intuited that to be both perfect *and* held in affection I needed an ideal Platonic family around me and this was to be a string quartet.

This ambition did actually work out, but of course when I first wished it I had no conception of just how complex and contradictory feelings can become between the members of a family.

Szymon Goldberg and the perfect up-bow

Since Manoug was old-fashioned enough to object to his pupils taking lessons or masterclasses with other teachers and I didn't want to upset him, I was discreet about playing for Szymon Goldberg at a Dartington Summer School one year. Goldberg was one of the outstanding talents of his era and a genuinely modest and delightful man.

At the age of only twenty he had been appointed concert-master of the Berlin Philharmonic under Wilhelm Furtwängler, who later saved him from the Nazis. When I met him he must have been about sixty. I knew nothing of his life but I instantly recognised his superb artistry and what I would describe as his quality of being. Following one wonderful lesson I asked him why he took time to listen to the student orchestra that I had assembled and was leading.

Arrogant young buck that I was, nearly all the other violinists, drawn from among my fellow students at the Royal Academy of Music, were attractive young women. Shamelessly I had invited them to Devon as prospective girlfriends.

Goldberg's reply was characteristically modest and to the point: 'I like to see who has a good vibrato – sometimes you see someone, even further back in the section, with a lovely natural, well-formed vibrato.'

I found this disconcerting as I still had a dreadful vibrato. The idea of listening for examples of good violin playing from the ladies of my orchestra had simply not occurred to me.

It was lunchtime and I was packing up as quickly as I could – I was always as hungry as a horse. I noticed Goldberg didn't seem to be getting ready to leave.

'Aren't you coming to lunch?' I asked. He looked so small, quiet and vulnerable, standing there with his beloved Guarnerius fiddle in his hands.

'No, I don't think so,' he said. 'I think I'll just do a little practice.'

Rather taken aback, I blurted out, 'But surely you don't need to practise more, from where *you* are?'

He looked deeply thoughtful, almost meek, then remarked quietly, 'Well, Paul, I find you can always do with a bit more practice!'

That evening at Dartington he gave a recital. He started with Webern's sparse Four Pieces, which opens with a single, long note played on an up-bow, starting with the right bowing arm fully extended and the tip of the bow on the string. The apparently simple gesture of gradually and smoothly 'drawing' the bow along its length by bringing the arm increasingly closer to the instrument is guaranteed to reveal the least self-doubt or tremor in a player. Professional violinists watch for such things in their peers because it is one of the most difficult techniques asked of them.

Irrespective of their level of virtuosity, nearly all performers crumple under the strain of such a revealing action and avoid tackling anything like it as an opening statement in a recital.

Goldberg came on stage already quietly focused and fully self-aware. He composed himself without any fuss and then – spaciously, without the slightest stress – positioned himself to perform this beautiful masterclass of a note. A single, pure, impossible note, perfectly executed.

In his hands and imagination it started from nowhere and gradually warmed up. It was a complete and glowing example of the art of vibrato. He began without any vibrato at all, gradually introducing a minimal finger vibrato in which only the top joint of the finger on the string becomes alive, then seamlessly transitioned into a warm and luscious wrist vibrato, loosening the wrist so that the hand oscillates, and finished with a thrilling arm vibrato.

I had never seen or heard anything remotely like it and indeed have never experienced its like again. It felt as if he had performed this feat just for me. I thank him for it from the bottom of my heart. It was an extraordinary example of understated perfection.

These things are among the most precious lessons of a musical life.

Alfred Brendel

At another concert during the Dartington Summer School, I observed the great pianist Alfred Brendel gather himself up in a similar manner immediately prior to playing a Beethoven sonata. I recognised with some awe that in the act of preparing to play he was internally mapping out the whole of his performance. I decided that this was the ideal I must learn to emulate.

I only dimly realised what a huge task I was setting myself. Mapping oneself out in a cool intellectual fashion is a tremendous achievement for anyone but it is doubly difficult for someone with a naturally warm, spontaneous, emotional nature.

Neville Marriner

One person who was always a friendly ally at the Royal Academy was Neville Marriner, then in the course of migrating from being a moderately effective fiddle player into an internationally renowned conductor.

I observed this – to me – questionable transition year by year during performances given by the Academy of St Martin in the Fields at Dartington.

In about 1967 I attended one of its early appearances when Neville introduced the ensemble as uniquely founded on entirely egalitarian principles. Its many fine instrumentalists were, he insisted, 'refugees from the restrictive commercial hierarchies of the established symphony orchestras'. He declared, 'We will always perform without leaders and above all will *never* under any circumstances suffer once more the indignities of following the dictates of any conductor.' They proceeded to give a wonderful and vibrant concert that was as inspiring as it was memorable.

The next year Neville was still playing on the front desk and directing the players from there, but all the solos were being played by the wonderfully gifted violinist Alan Loveday. How very sensible and grown up!

A couple of years later the orchestra was once again performing at Dartington. Neville stood up in order to explain that while it was an absolute axiom that they would never play under a conductor, they all felt that it was appropriate that they make some acknowledgement of the recent passing of Sir John Barbirolli, who for very many years had been the inspired conductor of the Hallé Orchestra.

I noticed Sir William Glock – then Director of the Dartington Summer School and, for the BBC, Director of the Music Programme and the Promenade Concerts – looking on approvingly. However, I thought some of the band looked less than happy.

As an ultimate concession Neville then placed an empty conductor's chair before the orchestra with a conductor's white baton placed across it and the ensemble played Wagner's *Siegfried Idyll* as a memorial.

The following year Neville could be found sitting in his familiar place, but now *without his violin*. He was now directing as presumably some kind of 'first among equals'. I began to feel a little less comfortable.

A season later Neville had graduated onto a raised podium and was conducting – but without a baton. No martinet he! Nonetheless I was distinctly queasy.

During the time I was leading the RAM chamber orchestra, Neville was our conductor. He was also flying each week between London and his new conducting post in Los Angeles.

Nearly every week he would take me aside in order to discuss the morality of being a conductor. This consisted mostly

of him seeking to justify himself. Although I found it difficult to articulate my disquiet, it was clear that he was only too
aware of my feelings. Despite my reservations regarding his
career path, I could not help liking Neville.

After a while he sought to recruit me into taking over the
Academy of St Martin in the Fields, insisting I take over the
conducting of the RAM chamber orchestra whenever he was
late, which he invariably was.

One week, with every sign of sincere concern, he asked me
whether I had been 'thrown out of the Royal Academy yet'.
I told him no. To which he replied, 'Well, you'd better get a
move on then, because no one makes a serious career until
they have!'

A few weeks later he prevailed on me as orchestral leader
to sit in with him to audition the violinists wanting to play in
the chamber orchestra. I was slightly taken aback but naturally flattered and so joined him one morning in order to sit in
judgement.

Rather awkwardly, the very first student to arrive was a nice
girl, who was or had been one of my girlfriends. I correctly
alerted Neville to the delicacy of the situation and he, equally
correctly, suggested I sit this one out.

To my slight discomfiture the next aspirant was another girl
I had been involved with and, to Neville's obvious delight, I
found myself sitting outside again. And so it went on.

By this stage Neville was beside himself with hilarity and
finally suggested that he read the complete list of those who
were due to turn up so that I could let him know if there were
any I *could* audition. As it turned out, to my embarrassment,
all but one were either current or recent girlfriends.

As he left for a rehearsal with the Academy of St Martin, I knew he was going to relish sharing this anecdote with the whole band.

By this late stage Neville had succeeded in persuading himself that it was an entirely natural and inevitable step for a musical director to use a baton: 'You must understand – if you don't the players at the back simply cannot see you.' I would see him staring through the door at me as I unwillingly took up the baton in his stead for the chamber orchestra rehearsals.

I continued to distrust any player who sought to 'master' his erstwhile colleagues. I had concluded that I was fundamentally suspicious of anybody who took it on themselves to be the arbiters of other people's feelings and emotions. I think this was a kind of conflation of my father's socialist beliefs and my own instincts. In any case, I had convinced myself that conducting was a form of emotional exploitation – and I still view it as such, particularly in terms of power and money.

Neville always insisted that it had been his dream to play in a string quartet and that he envied me the path I had taken. He even reiterated this one day many years later, when the quartet bumped into him in Hong Kong where we were playing and he – now with a knighthood and world famous – was about to conduct at the Festival.

Ironically, he probably had good reason to prod me towards the podium. Given my temperament perhaps I *should* have become a concerto-playing conductor. After all, what is the real moral distinction between manipulating other people's feelings by waving a stick at them rather than by coercing them through a violin?

Despite all Neville's charm and intelligence – or perhaps because of it – he did end up as masterful a manipulator and dictator as any of those conductors he denounced in his earlier idealistic days. And if I had followed his advice, I have no doubt I would certainly have become another baton-wielding monster.

Tradition

Exposure to such mature artists as Manoug Parikian, Szymon Goldberg, Sidney Griller and Neville Marriner made me increasingly aware of just how vital their various musical lineages were in shaping their approach, interpretation and sound production.

I gradually came to understand that every player carries an acquired musical 'history' that is painstakingly instilled and embodied via their teacher's sensibilities and disciplined tutelage, which in turn is informed by the teacher's own 'history'. This can often be detected by the informed listener, who learns to recognise those characteristic traits associated with particularly influential players.

The violin schools that have come down to us are probably as clearly differentiated as the various schools of painting and so on that continue to leave their mark on successive generations.

Respect for tradition is definitely not a feature of radical Marxism and I was never encouraged to feel connected to, still less to have any affection for, conventional traditional values. Yet when I came to marry I recognised how important it was to me that my wife had family traditions to follow, whereas – greatly though I admired their moral integrity – both my own parents were so radical in their beliefs that they had each been disowned by their families.

In life, an over-conservative observance of tradition slips easily into mere mechanical ritual, as it can in music or religious observance, and it is vitally important to strive to keep alive the essence of what we do rather than just the outward forms.

Two aspects of attention that help sustain such quality of function are dedication to personal excellence and working with and for others. Both require the help of a teacher or mentor, and reach fulfilment only when finally shared with a wider community.

The further I delve into the substance of my coma visions, the more convinced I become that above all our work with others is essentially a *moral* exploration by which we learn how best to express our relationship with our true Selves. This gradually extends our ability to acknowledge others, including our Maker, if we believe in a God. For our narrative of life to remain meaningful, this is surely the nature of the journey we must be making.

Some of this surreptitious respect for tradition was growing in me even despite my ignorance of it and must have been seeking expression in this next vision.

A survivor of Nagasaki

While I was unconscious, one of my visions involved experiencing a lengthy stay in a ghastly museum of dead – or nearly dead – survivors of Hiroshima and Nagasaki.

I am one of a small number of desperately emaciated and dying survivors of the nuclear bomb. The museum has parties of children and other visitors coming to observe our suffering, and our dreadful, grey lives consist of endlessly queuing to go from one room or laboratory to another. As we slowly move, pale and sick, between rooms we drag our feet in exhaustion. There are not many of us, maybe only twelve or so, and we are distinctly Japanese. The jailers or curators on the other hand are crude, loud-voiced Americans. There is a sense that the scenario also represents some kind of concentration camp.

Towards the end of this lengthy episode I first meet, and then briefly become, my wife's grandparents, who are evidently continuing their traditional occupations as fishermen but are doing so now in the radioactively polluted waters that surround their home. The fish they catch seem healthy but because of their poisoned environment they are impossible to sell. My wife's grandparents (who are sometimes also me but as far as I know were never fishermen) are very old, yet seem extraordinarily hale and energetic, although all their children have recently died from radiation sickness. They are sticking to their traditional lifestyle simply in order to prove that it is a legitimate way of life, even though the rest of the world has turned its back on it.

Although my wife's family is Japanese American, there is a great deal more being explored in this multilayered vision as it is overlaid with moral judgement and ambivalent emotion.

My wife's family has always impressed me in its stoicism and avoidance of negative emotion but, in my view, also seemed inclined towards a diplomatic and socially conventional attitude towards the world.

I rather blithely ascribed this restraint and politeness to a traditional Japanese family ethos and assumed the tendency towards discreet conservatism arose from a desire, shared by so many immigrants, to be assimilated into their adopted country – a particularly difficult task for the post-war Japanese community in the United States.

In retrospect, I am much less certain that this is what is being expressed in this vision. The reversal of roles – the older generation remaining fit while the young die – is perhaps a metaphor for America, as is the notion of being a tourist sight-seeing other people's misery. Sadly, such unsympathetic detachment is a common trait in those who hold power, or believe that they do. Yet taken at the level of personal psychology this is also an interesting way to regard the adult and the child that exist within each of us. The big issue is how to balance and nurture both aspects.

That the Japanese elders stay alive and support life by their connection to traditional values seems linked to other musical and cultural traditions that over the years have made a deep, unconscious impression on me.

I recall Manoug Parikian's affection and regard for his memories of simple craftsmen and of the great violinists he admired; Clifford Curzon's immense sensitivity towards the musical impressions and the values of his own early childhood; and Dr Roles's profound commitment to uphold the inner essence of the work of his teacher, P. D. Ouspensky . . .

A couple of years into my recovery a different theme came to the fore. This was a lengthy period of regret, self-appraisal and self-judgement. For many months I found myself unable to sleep because the nights were filled with painful personal recriminations. After a while I gave up trying to counter these feelings or seeking to hide them from myself – not that I could in any case. As the months passed I believe I replayed every single crude, gauche and selfish act of my life – and there were a great many of them.

This was not a familiar experience as I had previously always been inclined to smother feelings of guilt with action, ambition and bombast. These nights were wholly reflective and rendered all the more poignant by the recognition that none of these numberless acts of insensitivity could now be undone. This sensation of impotence was the hardest thing to come to terms with – yet why attend to things that can't be mended?

The process reached its apotheosis with an unexpected and heart-warming invitation to take up a fellowship in Berlin. The purpose was ostensibly in order to write this book, but living mostly entirely alone and with very little companionship encouraged an intense introspection, bordering on depression. I spent three months in this retreat and it was exactly what was needed. Certainly, until then I had had nothing to offer other people, even my beloved family.

One disturbing insight was the realisation that nothing I might have to contribute consisted of any of the qualities I had always assumed to be my special gifts. Gone was the dynamic decisiveness and domination and in its stead a quiet, passive, observing listener was peeking out. This shy creature was myself.

Gradually, the child who played the violin became visible again – the one who had retreated from the world into his love affair with the fiddle, modelling himself so much on his dad that he walked with a shambling anguished gait and who had even managed to mimic perfectly the tiny scratchy sounds of Kreisler's immortal 78 rpm recordings. Everything else was merely the carapace of personality.

I gradually realised that just as I had gone through a slow, extended near-death experience while ill and in coma, this withdrawal from the world was a form of attenuated self-judgment. Although it might not be fashionable to speak of such things, I am now convinced that judgement is a key part of dying. We might choose not to accept this and deny any such apocalyptic view of events, but I can attest to my own conviction that there *is* always a moral balance underlying our lives.

In common with many others who survive NDE, I am now absolutely intent on living without adding any further lies or unfinished business to my existence. Such accumulated deceit, especially self-deceit, proves a cruelly heavy burden when the call comes to travel lightly, as it must.

Forming the quartet

I assumed that if I gathered the best players of my generation, learned and thoroughly rehearsed the music, in time a seam-less homogeneous group would naturally emerge. I was all of nineteen years old, full of the arrogance of youth and – at least in my own eyes – highly gifted. I was confident that creating a perfect ensemble would be a relatively straightforward task.

A gifted fellow student, the viola player Paul Silverthorne, was putting together a mixed wind and string ensemble (including his oboist girlfriend) in order to perform works such as the Schubert Octet. He asked me to lead it.

I found learning and performing the octet boring and exhausting, but I did notice with interest the other string players Paul had chosen. With typical disregard for Paul and his girlfriend, I announced that I wanted Paul himself, together with violinist David Matthews and cellist Anthony Lewis (known as 'Lew') to become my new quartet.

Our early rehearsals were disturbingly unsuccessful. I would play as the music moved me but my new colleagues seemed incapable of staying with me – or even with each other. They sounded thin-toned and constantly out of tune. They generally had much less to play than I did and what they did have seemed extremely straightforward to me. With growing exasperation I realised that we would have to deal with each issue as it arose.

I began with the need to play together moment by moment ('ensemble'), but no matter how clearly I signalled my intentions my colleagues remained woefully adrift. And the gestures I was using to make my intentions clear disrupted my ability to play with the ease I normally enjoyed.

The alternative was to play strictly in time, but this rendered the musical phrasing mechanical and unnatural. When I tried to match my playing to the beat of a metronome I discovered that I was incapable of playing in time myself. This was so embarrassing that I tried to pretend it wasn't true.

I considered starting again with different players but it was obvious that these were the best the Academy had to offer. Since bullying and sarcasm weren't working, I decided I would have to cajole them into acquiescence. I concluded that all I could do was to trick them into believing I was their friend and hope that this would lead them to redouble their efforts to improve and respond to my needs. It seemed very tiresome.

As far as I could see they had only two main interests: going to the pub, which they did every lunchtime, and talking about sport – football or cricket, depending on the season. I had no familiarity with the concept of friendship, of belonging to a gang or a team. I had spent my childhood as a loner and had no desire to be anything else, but I decided a sacrifice was needed. One lunchtime I announced I would be joining them in the pub. They looked almost frightened but were too polite to demur and so this became our daily pattern.

It never crossed my mind to buy a round of drinks; why would I when I was there only to help them? In desperation I began to ask about their cricket teams. I couldn't bring myself even to try to discuss football, which to me seemed Neanderthal in the extreme!

By virtue of this assumed camaraderie I was gradually able to insinuate my own interests, including my ambitions for the group, into our conversations. What I didn't realise was that, with painful slowness, I was actually becoming a passable facsimile of a normal, social, human being.

I was constantly contriving to observe and manipulate my colleagues – or that's what I thought I was doing. Had the degree of detachment I sought and credited myself with been real, I would very likely have had to be regarded as autistic, or even sociopathic. Perhaps the truth was that, being over-sensitive and fundamentally shy, I needed to feel completely in control of any situation before I could ever trust myself to others.

Years later I became fascinated with the whole issue of leadership and concluded that my own starting place was neatly summarised in this beautiful little experiment by Konrad Lorenz.

Konrad Lorenz's fish

In Germany, just after the Second World War, the Nobel prize-winning biologist Konrad Lorenz published a delightful piece of research. He had been studying the way in which certain types of small fish bond together in large numbers to create the impression of being a single large entity, a phenomenon also observed in some flocks of birds and insect colonies. Creating the impression of being one large animal confuses possible predators and discourages attack.

Lorenz was struck by the extreme biological simplicity of the brain and nervous system of the species he was studying, which were so elementary that their sole purpose was the involuntary imitation of similar surrounding fish. Each individual fish is equipped with movement sensors on each side of its head to monitor its neighbour's changes of direction.

Lorenz was curious to discover what would happen if this simple brain were removed; this can be done without harming the creature. The result was that general functioning of the individual fish seemed in no way impaired – except that it no longer responded to the movement of the group. However, the lack of empathetic response meant this particular 'brain-less' fish became the leader of the shoal. This elegant experiment provides a delicious metaphor about how and why it is so often the socially unresponsive individual who becomes a leader.

Although I recognise myself as a compulsive leader, I am still obliged to acknowledge that – at this period in the development of the quartet – my single-minded personal agenda and almost complete disregard for my fellows' needs accounted for much of our earlier success. I might regret this more were it not that I know how well it worked for many years. While such dominance and certainty undoubtedly attracts many impressionable followers, it inevitably proves limiting to both individual and group evolution when it comes to working with increasingly developed colleagues.

In music, remarkably enough, there is an absolutely precise way of displaying this fracture line. Few choose to understand it intellectually, but the very best players recognise it intuitively and deal with it in practice every day of their working lives. It is known as the Pythagorean 'gap' or 'comma'.

The Pythagorean gap

This 'gap' accounts for the difficulties encountered even by accomplished musicians as they try to play in tune with each other. Ironically, the more accurate each individual's intonation, the greater the overall 'gap' between them.

The Pythagorean gap describes the *difference* of tuning between the notes of the scale, which arises from the natural harmonic series (which divide the string into ratios of 1:2, 2:3, 3:4 and so on) *compared* with the 12 chromatic semitones that result from tuning a succession of perfect fifths (i.e. $\frac{3}{2}$ to the power of 12).

Expressed mathematically:

7 perfect octaves contain 84 semitones (one octave $=$ 12 semitones).
This is equivalent to: $2^7 = 128$

Whereas 12 perfect fifths also contain 84 semitones (one 5th $=$ 7 semitones).
This is equivalent to $(\frac{3}{2})^{12} = 129.746337890625$

The ratio of these two (known as a 'comma' or 'gap') across the complete chromatic division of the octave is thus 1.013643264771.

For most of us this is not easy to understand aurally. An analogy might be that of the origami novice who seeks to fold his paper along precise lines only to discover that the more careful he is the more inexact the alignment of the corners becomes. In this case we can just about comprehend that this phenomenon occurs because each successive crease requires more paper across the folds.

A normal person accepts that it is exactly this imprecision that makes an object beautiful. But one of the things that makes human beings so interesting and quirky is that some of us carry on trying to achieve 'perfection' even when experience proves that it is not inherently achievable.

Like so many diligent spiders who will dedicate their whole life's energy to attempting to build a perfect web across the moving hands of a clock, 'artists' are destined to keep trying and failing, exercising their creativity within the tension between perfection and its own impossibility.

We are hard-wired to perceive too much asymmetry as 'ugly' but also find too little anodyne or boring. This is the aesthetic edge of the 'art of living'.

Complaining about this is as pointless as dismissing the miracle of a pearl as 'only a piece of unwelcome grit'.

Over the years I came to feel that the Pythagorean gap and all it represents was emblematic of the inevitable fractures and fault lines that characterise all group endeavour. Yet in time I also understood that the inescapable flaw at the heart of living and of creativity is the source of depth, integrity and beauty.

It is the constant tireless bridging of difference between people that gives rise to affection, whereas the common platitudes of hollow consensus result only in emptiness and superficiality.

The search for the perfect ensemble

To begin with I assumed that my colleagues in the quartet needed leadership. As decisiveness was my default position, I simply told them what to do, but although they were clearly willing to please me, this approach was a dismal failure. The more I dominated, the more impotent they became. And soon they were just sullen and joyless, which was musically – and personally – disastrous.

Only over many years did we gradually learn to accept that imperfection is the natural realm of possibility and, despite its frustrations, the vexed Pythagorean gap was itself a creative crucible. The struggle to resolve it instance by instance provided the necessary friction and energy to make us change.[*]

In this way the ensemble developed and matured. As leader I felt it was my role to strategise new creative tensions. I also insisted on exhaustive – perhaps almost obsessive – rehearsal, in order to be confident enough to be able to feel truly free in performance. The intensity of my risk-taking was related directly to the intensity of our preparation.

This particular approach was exercised within the narrow confines that classical music allows between freedom and control. Within this space, expressive perfection has to be created along a formal aesthetic 'cusp' – a narrow line that each of us had to negotiate with vigilance and dedication.

Over the years I came to see that this creative edge, which in the larger scale of things also represents free will, is itself a product of the Pythagorean gap, when applied to psychological domains for which there is as yet no reliable calibration or exact measurement.

Finding expressive freedom through infinite attention to detail is one thing, but taking liberties without regard for others or one's own deep conscience is something quite different. It may be unfashionable to say so, but there is a price

---

[*] This is also literally true of our Western musical system where it is the gap, expressed as sharps, flats and naturals, that we use to modulate, i.e. to change key.

for everything in this world and we must take care that we never make others pay for our personal preferences or supposed 'needs'.

'Tempering'

By painstaking adjustment and compromise in individual tuning while playing together it is just about possible to reconcile the Pythagorean gap. In music this is called 'tempering', but it also tests the psychological 'temperament' of the players themselves.

Bach succeeded in creating a practical, mathematical easing of the Pythagorean gap, which at the time was sorely needed for the tuning of mechanical church organs. He called his method 'tempering' and showcased the efficacy of his system in his ground-breaking *Well-Tempered Clavier*.

In so doing he paved the way for our modern 'tempered' tuning systems in which the gap is distributed equally across all the notes of the chromatic scale. This means that the modern piano is actually always slightly out of tune but so discreetly so that most listeners do not register it. On the other hand, it could well be that our modern sensitivity to pitch has become so degraded that we do not notice what would once have been heard as an unacceptable distortion.

Unfortunately, such approximation is simply inadequate for anything but the crudest string quartet playing – although this does not seem to stop many otherwise proficient groups from using it. There are also a number of other tempting options that avoid having to face up to these tensions.

Young quartets often resort to having an over-dominant first violin acting as soloist, while the other three players become a subservient support group. This approach is completely inappropriate to the essential properties of string quartet playing, which is designed to be a meeting of equals, although at times one player will need to be 'more equal than others'.

Another unsatisfactory approach – often the resort of orchestral players – is to use a constant over-generous vibrato. Although this is superficially impressive, ultimately it removes vital tensions from the quartet – much like making curry without chillies. The masterpieces of the string quartet repertoire in performance communicate the challenges and uglinesses of relationship as well as its joys and consolations.

The only honourable route for any serious quartet is to take pains over mediating each tonal gap as it occurs. This ensures transparency while engaging a quite different order of awareness. Each member has to recognise that for the ensemble to take wing it is necessary to compromise personal sensibilities by carefully playing 'out of tune' for the greater good.

Moral authority and leadership lies with the person willing to be in error for the benefit of others. The example of Christ's sacrifice comes to mind, but the deep wisdom of many other spiritual traditions is psychologically illumined by this perception.

The issue of 'temperament' has parallels with every technical aspect of performance, including tempo, sonority, rhythm, dynamics and phrasing, and its resolution becomes pervasive and engrossing – and above all time-consuming. Along the way we discover that it not only involves the external qualities of what we do but also requires a radical retuning of our own personal temperament and habitual personality. From that point onwards we are beginning to deal with really essential issues.

Although he never put it in these terms, our quartet coach at the Royal Academy, Sidney Griller, an eminent leader himself, always insisted that 'a quartet doesn't even begin to exist until it has been playing together for at least ten years – and even then it should not attempt Beethoven until it has been going for fifteen years'.

Until one has reached the level of being and understanding needed in order to become both servant and master within a group, nothing 'real' can be achieved. The process is a kind of alchemy.

Personal perfection

Throughout all my medical crises and while I was in coma facing death, my principal concern was 'Who am I?' This question, which is as old as time, took on a new level of urgency as I increasingly lost all customary sense of myself.

To a certain extent the way the answers presented themselves changed their nature, but the one question that remained throughout was 'Can I truly exist alone or only through my relationships with others?'

For instrumentalists, this dilemma is played out in becoming either a soloist or an ensemble player. Irrespective of which path we follow, we gradually learn that perfection cannot lie in any one single approach. Dedicated personal practice and exhaustive group rehearsals are equally vital in building a creative identity, just as psychologically healthy individuals must usually seek fulfilment in relationships with others.

Personal and relationship breakdowns are inevitable in life and it is often through these crises that we discover the depth of our emotional resources. Existential threats might demand radical adaptation and change in order to re-establish the relative equilibrium we call recovery. Along the way, what remains of our past and what we take into the future is reordered and thrown into sharper focus. Following the threat to my very existence, embodied by collapse and illness, my principal preoccupation has been to learn to accept that all such paradox is inevitably self-constructed.

Our perception of the world might be enhanced and given perspective by our having two eyes, two ears and two brain hemispheres, but this does not mean that either the inner or the outer world is intrinsically dualistic or bicameral. Once we learn to 'get out of the way of ourselves', we find that ambivalence and paradox are the only ways we can perceive and penetrate further into this 'conscious' universe, vast and rich beyond imagining.

Since it is solely our limited thinking that causes us to polarise issues into apparently irreconcilable contradictions, it is not surprising that my coma visions never supported any such one-dimensional notions. At the end of everything lies silence – the ultimate paradox, and its ultimate resolution. The approach to silence becomes ever deeper and increasingly richly imbued with meaning, making it all the more engrossing and beautiful. At this level beauty lies beyond definition – closer perhaps to the pure union of love or perfection.

The husky

I was a dog in the Arctic tundra, one of a group of huskies drawing a sledge and sometimes leading the team. Everything felt utterly physically real. I was running around on all fours and had rough, hairy skin. When I was leading the pack as the front-runner I was exhilarated, but felt equally thrilled within the pack as I followed the dog in front of me nose to tail.

Apart from brief stops to rest or eat we were nearly always wearing the traces for drawing the sledge, but towards the end of this Arctic adventure I found myself free of the harness – running tirelessly and boisterously across the snowy terrain in the way that dogs do.

In most dreams in which we become someone else we tend to observe ourselves from outside but this was not the case here. I *was* a dog; I thought and acted like one and my existence was entirely canine. Dogs figure prominently in many ancient religions, sometimes acting as emissaries of healing or as guides into the afterlife. This vision had a shamanistic or archetypal quality.

When I was very young we had a large and boisterous dog that used to knock me over. I now have no memory of this but I am still frightened of dogs and generally dislike them. This dream sequence could represent the overcoming of unconscious fears, but I believe it also represents a mammalian 'memory' of what it means to be simultaneously leader and part of the pack – the role of the first violin in a string quartet.

Despite my habitual distrust of dogs, the overwhelming pleasure of being one lay in the sense of freedom and untrammelled instinct – precisely those impulses we most subjugate in order to be 'civilised', and a perfect image for a life in music.

As a dog there was much I could not understand, but I was very aware of the drivers, clean-shaven, dominant men, all of whom were extremely muscular and smelled strongly of unpleasantly crude aftershave. I never saw these figures in full, just their lower limbs and an occasional forearm – which I suppose makes sense for a bedridden patient or a dog. How I came to sense any of this when I was meant to be comatose remains a mystery.

Throughout this sequence I was very aware of extreme changes of temperature. There was snow on the ground and a little house set on a whitened hillside, even at one stage a bizarre snowman and some Christmas lights, but fortunately, even in the deep midnight frost, I had a thick furry coat to keep me warm.

Few people have become a dog, apart from the odd shaman or lycanthrope. As I write this I remember a strange short story by Franz Kafka, entitled *Investigations of a Dog*, which I read too young and which had the same disquieting effect on me as my first reading of Gurdjieff. The canine protagonist of Kafka's novella spends his time trying to work out his relationship to God, but never gets beyond the point of believing in some mystical relationship between his eating, defecating and then miraculously being given food again.

The central problem is that he can never grasp the notion that there are actually other entities, such as people, involved in his existence. There is only himself and God. Because of this narrowed perception he is simply unable to register human beings or to recognise the connection between them and the 'miraculous' provision of his food.

The dog's situation was just the same as my own while I was in coma, unable to recognise the function of the nurses or my relationship to them and mostly not even seeing them. But even this represented a significant advance from my initial condition, in which I had no sense of 'existing' at all.

According to some mystic traditions my changing levels of consciousness could be seen as mimicking an evolutionary path from mineral to vegetable and then on through simple life forms until finally I reached a rudimentary animalistic awareness. I speculate that during the period just prior to reawakening I was indeed functioning as an animal.

It is difficult to know to what extent my changing physical condition influenced the content of my visions – and vice versa. This was one of the last visions I had before returning to consciousness but there was no question of my being unable to move my doggy limbs; quite the contrary. My actual paralysis could have generated dreams of being unable to move but while I was a dog I was running around freely on all fours, although the breathless exertions of the dream might also have related to the laboured breathing brought on by attacks of tachycardia. Similarly, the bitterly cold Arctic setting and the extremes of hot and cold might have reflected the feverish symptoms of repeated infections.

This extended sequence was suddenly, violently and most incongruously interrupted by the faces of my wife and daughter ripping the sky asunder and peering down on me in order to tell me that I was going to be fine and that all was well. Deep in my dogginess, I found these loving visitors intrusive and unwelcome. Their intervention felt shocking and inappropriate, as if a couple of deities had suddenly dropped in unexpectedly for tea or if some utterly engrossing childhood game had been cavalierly disrupted by loud and insensitive grown-ups.

The transition from childhood to early adulthood follows a similar path: vital and inevitable in the formation of our identity, but often confusingly unwelcome. Professional musicians retain a distinctive infantilism and together with other gifted fantasists – such as actors and card sharps – devote as much of their lives as they can to 'playing'.

Launching the quartet

As soon as it was clear to me that this quartet was going to be my career, I began to plan the repertoire and how to make an impact with our performances.

The choice of work was relatively straightforward because above all I desperately wanted to play Janáček's Second Quartet, 'Intimate Letters'. I had heard the climax one day on the radio – not the whole piece, just the searing, screaming climactic passage of erotic ecstasy that rips through the otherwise beguiling and placid third movement.

I had never heard music like this before and it filled my body with a thrilling rush of arousal. While it was playing I couldn't breathe, move or think, and once it was over I was shell-shocked and only gradually returned to life.

I bought the music as soon as I could and we set about it. It was unthinkably difficult, bizarre and unconventional.

Through the many years of rigorous scale practice I had undertaken under the scrupulous tutelage of Manoug Parikian, the only scales he had ever been lax about were those in sixths. 'Don't bother about those,' he said when I raised the question. 'I've never once had need to play sixths in my career and they certainly don't feature in any concertos.'

I was unconvinced and so discreetly continued my diligent practice of all the many scales and arpeggios as laid out by the pedagogic violin master Carl Flesch in his authoritative, encyclopedic *Scalensystem*.

The opening passages of this bizarre and unconventional masterpiece consist entirely of melodies in sixths – and even with all my previous preparation they were still virtually unplayable. In fact so was the whole piece.

Despite this – or perhaps because of it – I instinctively understood everything about it musically. Up to this time my response to music had been entirely intuitive and fundamentally 'ignorant' – at least in the sense that I had no interest in engaging any cognitive or 'learnt' process on how to listen. In this I was, as Beecham facetiously remarked, very like 'the British who may not like music but they absolutely love the noise it makes'.

Much as I did love the sound of music, particularly the violin, what I found completely irresistible was the emotion that certain passages of music could evoke in me.

The Amadeus Quartet (who by then I had regularly heard perform at the Dartington Summer School) could always melt my heart when they played Schubert. But I have to admit that I didn't really appreciate Schubert at all apart from the specific moments and passages of heightened emotion. To me all the rest of it was merely the price one had to pay for those instants of utter delight.

Although one of the first quartets we ever learned and performed was the lovely one in A minor (D. 804), the 'Rosamunde', it was not until the very end of our career that we were able to perform and record a really authoritative version of what I consider to be Schubert's greatest quartet, the G major (D. 887), and this was possible only because by then we

Tuning violin: Paul aged 9 (*right*), Oxford Town Hall (1962)

Paul aged about 15

Kingham Hill School Choir, 1960s,
Paul front row, sixth from right

With mum Tessa, dad John and Chika (1981)

The family at Dartington (1987): *left to right*, John, Paul, Caspian, Tessa, Thaïs, Chika

THE MEDICI QUARTET

As a young ensemble (*c.*1974), *left to right*, founder members:
Paul Robertson (violin 1), David Matthews (violin 2),
Paul Silverthorne (viola), Anthony Lewis (cello)

In 1982: David Matthews, Ivo-Jan van der Werff,
Anthony Lewis, Paul Robertson

Manoug Parikian (*left*) with David Oistrakh

Clockwise from top left: Sir Clifford Curzon, Dr Francis Roles,
Szymon Goldberg, Professor Richard Guyatt

Paul and Chika performing Bartók duos in their barn (2000)

THE MEDICI QUARTET

Celebrating the auction at the Queen Elizabeth Hall, 1985,
from left to right: David Matthews (2nd violin), Paul, Michael Willis Fleming,
Tony Lewis ('Lew') cellist, unknown, Ivo-Jan van der Werff (viola), Alan Mann.

Playing for the TV series, *Music and the Mind*, 1996

Paul with Sir John Tavener following performances of
Towards Silence in Salisbury Cathedral, 2011

had been utterly saturated by the architectural grandeur of the Beethoven quartets that are its inspiration.

Janáček 2

Fortunately for me Janáček's unique quartet steps around these issues, because it consists entirely of a sequence of highly charged moments with none of that boring intellectual 'chuntering about' linking them together. Perfect!

Another attraction for me was that the Janáček 'Intimate Letters' quartet – originally entitled 'Love Letters' – was inspired by the stream of love letters that flowed between the seventy-four-year-old composer and his mistress, the bewitching young Kamilla Stösslová, some thirty-five years his junior. The besotted composer composed the whole work on scraps of manuscript, each of which distilled the emotion of one of these passionate letters.

His final act was to retreat into his study while he struggled to bring these musical letters together as a coherent composition. When he emerged he was clearly dying. The first performance took place with his long-suffering widow sitting on one side of the hall while his mistress was sitting across the aisle.

All of this spoke to me in a very particular way because I was deeply drawn to the notion that such thrilling music might inhabit an uninhibited, untrammelled world all of its own, as it did for me. I was also fascinated that emotion, particularly sexual emotion, might have its own special language and form. This meant that such heightened physicality had its own legitimacy.

I felt this was at least a tacit recognition of the 'magical' world of music – somewhere far beyond the reach of ordinary thinking, still less of rational explanation.

Although I was perfectly fluent verbally, I was always deeply distrustful of language, which seemed to me to be suspiciously malleable and subject to wilful distortion and manipulation – in other words, lying. Because of this I took great care to keep my musical instincts far away from what I saw as the hyper-cleverness of intellectualism, analysis or theorising.

This division of personal response continues to this day, although over the years I have observed an interesting natural 'suturing' of the untutored instinctive and intuitive into other, more coherent forms of understanding.

An illustration of this curious internal embargo is that early on I discovered that the only way I could read music was kin-aesthetically. In other words, when I looked at notes on a stave I deciphered them solely through their associated hand shapes on the violin and it was only these internally imagined finger shapes that told me what the music would actually sound like.

Although there are obvious drawbacks to this approach, I remained surprisingly attached to it because it meant that my relationship to the symbolic representations of printed notes on a stave had to be grounded in physicality.

In this manner the dichotomies between my mother's essential practicality and my father's abstract representations of the world could be held in an internal balance. Since I wanted both, I somehow unconsciously constructed this curious contrary dynamic within myself in relation with the *body* of the violin and its '*heady*' musical aspirations.

Another feature of my embodied musicality was that it obliged me to commit to extreme rehearsal regimes. This was certainly exhausting, particularly for my colleagues, whom I could trust only by way of infinitely painstaking repetition. Later on I found at least one like-minded performer in the person of Clifford Curzon, whom I now believe shared an exactly similar fundamental lack of trust, not of the music but of other people.

Therefore I made everyone in the quartet work through each and every phrase and gesture of Janáček's Second Quartet, in just the same way that a dedicated person might seek to discover the meaning of a foreign language through endless repetitions of its phonetic sounds.

Curiously enough, we succeeded. After about two years we could give a thrilling and uniquely 'authentic' performance of this powerful and idiosyncratic work.

I began to contemplate doing something that at that period no one did any more: to present a formal debut concert in the Wigmore Hall. At the time this once lovely chamber music hall was at a nadir in its fortunes. It was shabby, downtrodden and neglected. But it still had its history.

We took advice about what other works to programme. I think it was Derek Simpson, the wonderful cellist of the Aeolian Quartet, who proposed the Ravel quartet. Interestingly, even our awkward and moody quartet teacher at the Royal Academy of Music, Sidney Griller, cautiously agreed.

Griller was a difficult man to love, although I admired much about him. He came across as distant, bitter and facetious but he was clearly no fool. His own quartet had enjoyed a first-rate career and endured a catastrophic final breakdown, by which time he was a covert drinker. He and I always shared some kind of unspoken intimacy. I think he must have been as much a bastard leading as I was!

Ravel

While the Janáček quartet speaks to the big 'driving' muscles deep inside, full of masculine power and naked sexuality, the Ravel might seem facile or effeminate by contrast. But to think this would be a mistake.

Ravel's only string quartet is a svelte, polished, sensuous masterpiece best summarised by the composer himself, who once responded to the criticism that his music was 'artificial' by wittily commenting, 'What some people don't seem to appreciate is that some of us are *naturally* artificial!'

The exquisite colours and subtle palette of this composition might contrive to persuade us of its superficiality, but in fact the work is entirely classical, even Mozartian in conception: perfectly formed and beautifully balanced in both structure and sensitivity. The work may be skin deep – but what silky skin! It positively reeks with sex hormones.

Although we did not perhaps appreciate it at the time, this score is very pleasing to audiences and encourages the players to explore the most refined vocabulary of musical finesse.

We were already making a fair fist of it when the Aeolian Quartet generously invited us to attend a coaching course they were running at Roedean School in Brighton.

Although I was always snootily contemptuous of their leader Emanuel ('Manny') Hurwitz's playing, he was as generous as his kind colleagues in showing us how to transform our merely adequate rendition into an outstanding one.

Manny took me aside one lunchtime and gave me the keys to unlocking the piece. He carefully explained how essential it was to accelerate my bow speed and lighten my touch on the strings in order to create a translucent sonority. Once I 'got' it this simple device transformed the piece.

We were immediately able to work through the quartet, pointing up each tonal and dynamic colour combination and dynamic. Indeed it wasn't long before we were, in truth, performing it better than our teachers did. When he heard us play it, dear Manny looked simultaneously equally elated and deflated.

Manny was a walking encyclopaedia when it came to violins, bows, music and string quartets – all things musical in fact. He also had a wry Jewish humour in which the truth is revealed with an almost painful irony.

I recall him solemnly informing me that all string quartets had the same basic line-up: 'one good violinist, one bad violinist, one failed violinist and one person who hates all violinists'!

On another occasion he asked me whether I knew how to become a millionaire as a string quartet player. Genuinely intrigued, I shook my head. 'Do you know, Paul?' he enquired again and then answered his own question with delight: 'It's easy. Start as a billionaire!'

It must have been at about then, 1972 or thereabouts, that I had my big 'bust-up' with Manoug Parikian. Things came to head when he very angrily informed me that he had absolutely no interest in my becoming a quartet player and that furthermore he strongly disapproved of it.

By this time I had been his stalwart and obedient pupil for six or seven years and had never missed a single lesson or questioned his authority. I explained that my quartet was currently giving numerous performances for the Royal Academy of Music, which was at the time celebrating its 150th anniversary.

Hearing this, Manoug replied to the effect that 'all I expect of you is that you turn up with the movement or movements of whatever concerto I have given you to learn and play it'! After much thought I concluded that Manoug was expecting me to turn up for a lesson only when I was thus prepared and so I decided to give my next lesson a miss.

The following week the registrar (the same one who had laughed so heartily during my fight with the rude conductor) came up to me, clearly very concerned. In his office he read me the letter of complaint that Manoug had sent him. In it he said that 'Robertson had behaved most rudely by not coming to his lesson' and was therefore 'insubordinate'!

Was there ever such a mammoth storm in such a piddling little tea cup? And was there any language more likely to alienate me than this quasi-military nonsense?

The registrar begged me to apologise, which I adamantly refused to do. He then urged me to reach some kind of accommodation, as without Manoug's agreement the Academy could not even allocate me to another teacher. I refused this also.

A couple of weeks later dear Manny Hurwitz took me aside in order to understand the situation better. Once he did, he passed a few unflattering comments about Manoug and generously offered to give me free lessons for the rest of my time as a student. Arrogant bugger that I was, I barely thanked him and it was only much later that I woke up to just what a kind and supportive action this was. Thank you, Manny.

Having settled on two showcase pieces for our planned Wigmore debut, all that remained was to come up with a full final programme. At this juncture even Sidney Griller grudgingly agreed to the plan, merely insisting that we start with a Haydn string quartet, without which, as he quite correctly pointed out, we could not be taken seriously.

We prepare for our Wigmore Hall debut

I booked the Wigmore Hall and my dear father took it on himself to write to all the London churches offering them free lunchtime performances of our programme.

In all, eighteen churches accepted and we spent the whole of the summer of 1973 performing our Haydn–Janáček–Ravel programme at a series of free concerts.

One of these turned out to be of particular significance. All Souls', Langham Place, is an attractive neo-classical church directly opposite the BBC's Broadcasting House. We were such novices that I remember our being quite nervous in case someone from the BBC happened to come along.

By some oversight our concert was scheduled to begin at 12.15 p.m., while all the other concerts in the series started at 1 p.m. As a result, when we were ready to start, the audience in the church consisted of three tramps and a dog. A hasty consultation took place between us in which I maintained that we should play regardless. Not surprisingly, my colleagues were not so enthusiastic, but I insisted that we were not playing to please an audience but in order to prepare ourselves.

It is always somewhat dispiriting for a string quartet to outnumber its audience, but when even such audience as there is are all fast asleep on the back pews, it is difficult to feel musically uplifted. To be fair, the dog made every effort to remain awake during the Haydn quartet, but even he succumbed half-way through the slow movement. Perhaps he preferred Bach.

We went through the awkward ritual of briefly leaving the stage between the first two works and returned to start the impassioned Janáček quartet accompanied by the sound of distant stentorian alcoholic snoring.

Having finally duly completed our performance of the Ravel, we didn't bother to go offstage to change out of our suits. After all, who was going to see?

None of us exchanged a word – there was nothing left to say. As we were each consumed by our own sombre thoughts, from behind a pillar where he had been hiding stepped a well-groomed man in an elegant suit.

He came over with a friendly smile and extended his hand in a warm handshake. 'Hello,' he said. 'My name's Eric Thomson and I'm the Deputy Director of the Arts Council.'

Ignoring our various states of undress but indicating the deserted church, he continued, 'I'm really impressed by what I've seen today and I'd like to help you.' With that he gave me his card and, having made me promise to call him, he left.

Dear Eric was as good as his word. Within days he had arranged for us to receive a grant to support us through the rest of the summer and he remained a true friend for very many years.

At last, on 31 October 1973, our debut concert was upon us.

Our debut concert

We were naturally terrified, even though by then we had already received a wonderful write-up in the *Manchester Guardian* from their senior music critic, Gerald Larner, who had reviewed our very first professional concert at the Harrogate Music Festival.

The Wigmore Hall was packed. Dad had written to every-one he could think of to invite them to attend and at the last moment the Worshipful Company of Musicians supported the evening with a block booking.

Glancing out I could see the diminutive figure of Sidney Griller bobbing up and down in his seat alternately trying to hide and then desperately elevating himself in order to see past the patrician figure of the large lady sitting immediately in front of him.

Time passed both far too fast and endlessly slowly. My fin-gers seemed constantly out of control and all the difficult tech-nical passages felt like being launched down the Cresta Run without a sleigh. At the same time my bow seemed to have taken on a life of its own – a serpentine wriggly life. I prayed it would stay on the string long enough to play the sustained melodies. Such are performance nerves.

When we finished there was much cheering and clearly an encore was called for. Fortunately we had one prepared, the witty finale of Haydn's Op. 33 No. 2, 'The Joke'.

By the time we came to play it I had hardly any control left and we had not really had much opportunity to get used to playing an encore in front of an audience – even the tramp's dog had stopped wagging his tail long before an encore would have been called for.

Still, we scraped by.

The following day, 1 November, was my twenty-first birthday. It was curiously memorable because I spent it entirely alone. No one called and none of my girlfriends showed up.

The papers hadn't yet printed any reviews of the concert so I had no way of knowing whether our concert was going to be considered a critical success. The following day all the serious papers gave us rave reviews. We were launched.

Within weeks of our debut we were signed up by the daunting and formidable Emmy Tillett, Director of Ibbs and Tillett, the country's foremost music agents. Emmy quickly moved to shape our future, arranging a job for us at York University and a prestigious recording contract with EMI. A few weeks later we found ourselves with a full diary and performances booked all over the UK for music clubs and festivals.

Two mentors

During this period I was fortunate enough to come under the influence of two great men, each outwardly very different but undoubtedly seeking the same truth by different paths. One was an elderly doctor, Francis Roles, and the other, also elderly, the English pianist, Sir Clifford Curzon.

Sir Clifford Curzon

A few months after our debut, Emmy Tillett called to tell me that she had arranged for us to play with Sir Clifford, one of her most illustrious artists, and by then one of the world's leading musicians.

This proved to be one of my most significant, life-changing relationships.

At almost exactly the same time a whole series of events unfolded that finally led me to meet my other great mentor, Dr Francis Roles.

Despite their many differences, I loved and revered both these remarkable men because their lives exemplified what they taught and held to be true. Their influence was to accompany me into the afterlife during my illness and ensuing coma.

Dr Roles used to say that when we leave this world we carry remarkably little with us and that the great secret of life lies in discovering that 'we have nothing of our own'. In my twenties I listened intently to these words and endeavoured to absorb their truth – but I was too young and certainly too egotistical to grasp their true meaning. I now understand them quite differently and can even elaborate a little from personal experience.

Guarding your talent: 'Know thyself'

Even as I was forging links with Dr Roles, the quartet had the extraordinarily good fortune to be formally taken under the tutelage of Sir Clifford Curzon.

Over the next few years he set about trying to shape us into real artists and very generously devoted much of his energy to me. There was never any doubt as to who was the senior partner, for Clifford was universally revered throughout the musical world.

The long days spent in rehearsal were a mixture of torture and wonder. It seemed that each revelation could be achieved only by some kind of sacrifice or at personal cost.

143

As well as being a unique musical master, Clifford was charming, complex and paradoxical. He was also something I most emphatically was not: a 'gentleman'. Clifford was polished in everything, including his dress and his manners, but, more importantly, in his culture, education and bearing.

I discovered in the course of writing this book that his German – Jewish? – family name, Siegenberg, was changed at the outbreak of the First World War. Although I had no knowledge of it at the time, Clifford was arguably yet another foreign Anglophile. When I mentioned that I was Jewish, Clifford did tell me how proud he was of having a Jewish grandmother.

He set us inflexible rules. We were to arrive at his grand house in leafy Highgate at precisely 9 a.m. each morning and rehearse until exactly eleven o'clock, when we would move from the studio to the elegant drawing room where he served coffee, laid out by his housekeeper.

At 11.30 a.m. we would return to the studio and work again until one o'clock when he politely but firmly turned us out of the house while he had lunch and took a nap. We returned at 2.30 p.m. to rehearse until 5 p.m., with a formal tea break each afternoon at 3.30 p.m.

This 'afternoon tea', which took place in the drawing room with its fine collection of early French Impressionists, became the setting for my ritual humiliation. Clifford was insistent that I learn every nuance of the English 'tea ceremony', which is of course every bit as tortuous and formal as its Japanese counterpart. For the uncouth plebeian that I was, brought up in a caravan with neither money nor culture, such a social ritual was alien and incomprehensible.

Clifford set about training me with commendable patience and a certain malicious glee. Under his critical scrutiny I would sit perilously on one of his delicate eighteenth-century chairs, balancing one of his precious eighteenth-century porcelain tea cups, while attempting to act out the numerous demands of this (to me) outmoded English upper-class ritual.

Waiting until I had managed at last to get close to having a first gulp of tea, Clifford would suddenly lunge forward to offer me a scone, home-baked in his kitchen. Without any noticeable effort he would invariably contrive to present the plate so that he proffered me the single, unfortunate 'runt' of the batch. Seeing me hesitate, he would say, 'Paul, you do know that good manners dictate that you must take the scone nearest you on the plate. As a gentleman, you *do* know that, don't you, Paul?'

Cowed, I would duly take the one scone that had failed to rise evenly. Feigning to ignore my anxiety he would turn to engage my colleagues in polite, inconsequential chit-chat. They all seemed to find this highly amusing, although, like naughty prep-school boys, much of their good humour stemmed from a cowardly relief that it was not they who were the butts of similar attention.

As if addressing them, Clifford would then explain how in polite society it was unthinkable ever to take a knife to the scone. Oh no! Apparently, 'good manners' dictated that the scone be first placed on the snowy-white damask tablecloth alongside the dainty tea plate. Then, and only then, could one use the knife to lift out just the right, modest amount of butter and jam, which were to be placed at the edge of the plate, just so. Only then, and using only the fingers, could the scone, carefully suspended above the table, be elegantly divided and the two perfect halves placed on the plate. Only at this juncture was it possible to apply the butter and jam.

With further feigned fatherly kindness he would watch the others each fulfil this seemingly simple task and then invite them all to join him in observing me. Of course, my misshapen freak of a scone would inevitably resist all attempts at such a division, only to burst asunder in an explosion of crumbs. At this point Clifford would utter a stifled, derisory 'Mmphh!'

Carefully averting his eyes, he then proceeded to offer various 'helpful' prompts, writhing in theatrical contempt as I inevitably fell at each successive hurdle. When at last, in desperation, I picked up a squashy bundle of collapsed scone, vaguely topped with a blob of runny butter and some sticky jam, would he turn and sweetly inform me that 'of course the art of taking tea is to engage in elegant and diverting conversation as you are having it'. Having delivered this withering line and assuming an air of disappointment, he would pull a mock-sour face to my colleagues.

My deflation complete, we would then repair back to the studio where the suffering continued, but taking a rather different form, because here, alongside the misery, there were always moments of wonderful insight and beauty.

I have dwelt on this seemingly trivial scene because it is forever etched on my mind as an essential memory of Clifford, my beloved teacher and mentor. Apparently based on a long outdated and (to me) demeaning Edwardian ritual, this peculiar mixture of understated, old-fashioned, critical playfulness, over-demanding perfectionism and guarded intimacy is exactly what he brought to his peerless playing and it became what I afterwards continually sought in my own performances and person.

These elaborate formal 'afternoon teas' remained painfully humiliating to me but the prize for suffering through them was that after the close of proceedings, Clifford would invite me to stay behind and have a quite different, entirely informal cup of tea, and a chat. These conversations became one of the highlights of our relationship and also some of my most cherished memories. I miss them still.

In the intimate conversations we enjoyed after the long torrid days of rehearsal and struggle, we discussed all kind of things about which a young man seeks wise counsel: the purpose of life, the nature of musical talent, reincarnation, sex and love and so on.

We had an unspoken understanding that in these private conversations, and only then, I was free to ask him questions about any topic that interested me.

Once I asked him what he felt was the artist's highest duty. It was clearly something he had spent a lot of time thinking about and his response was particularly thoughtful and articulate. After a moment's consideration he replied, 'The artist's highest responsibility is to learn how to guard his talent.'

At that time I naively believed that Clifford was oversensitive and 'temperamental', and in my youthful ignorance I assumed he was referring to the many slights and pressures of the musical world – fans, agents, critics and all the other external demands that crowd in on a performer's life. But I now feel that he was also referring to the far more urgent need to defend oneself from the pervasive, destructive forces of petty personal hubris, which in the final analysis underlies most of our supposed misfortune.

Although occasionally risqué, Clifford was never vulgar and he was immensely reflective and subtle in his thinking. I recall how disarmingly honest he became when I was telling him about my parents. He listened intently and then to my surprise said with the utmost sincerity, 'I see you are more spiritually developed than I am.' I was aghast and rather shocked to hear such a thing from him and could say nothing. But I noted with huge pleasure that when he first met my mother, in Malvern where we were playing, he stood up and insisted on graciously holding her hand, charming her with the sort of gallantry normally reserved for royalty. I was deeply touched, particularly as my mother's poor old hands were so gnarled and disfigured. He was a blessed man.

Looking back, I can see that above all he was imbued with an exquisite, fastidious and almost feminine sensitivity, both vulnerable and deeply kind. These refined qualities were present in his sound, which was uniquely tender and fluid. He was sensitive, reflective and wonderfully tender, everything a 'developed' man should be.

On one occasion during one of our precious end-of-day teas he said, 'You really hate those afternoon teas, don't you?'

'Yes,' I answered.

He looked so thoughtful and kind. 'You do know that I'm only doing it to help you, don't you?' he said tenderly.

'Yes, I know.'

And, oddly enough, I did.

Towards the end of our relationship I realised that Clifford was dying, although for a long time he hid it with his customary care and discretion. He generally avoided teaching and made it clear he had no wish to share his insights with players who, in his words, 'would steal his secrets'. In so many ways it was my great good fortune to become his apprentice.

As his illness progressed, his awesome technical command and control began to slip away. A lesser player might have been content to settle for mere adequacy but Clifford clearly could not bring himself to capitulate so easily and insisted on sticking to his rigorous, almost neurotically obsessive and exhausting rituals of preparation.

Sadly, such over-rehearsal simply became too much for his diminishing energies, and towards the end our rehearsals often held more magic than our actual performances. Just once, when we had learned and performed the Elgar Piano Quintet together, everything went just the way it was meant to and his full genius was revealed.

I felt entirely inadequate to find a way to thank him properly, although I was still sufficiently immature to be embarrassed by all the wrong notes he played. As it turned out, our performance of Dvořák's Piano Quintet with him in 1982 proved to be his very last.

Even in his intense physical misery he played the opening chords of the slow movement with such a miraculous beauty that it wrung the heart. How he could manage this when at death's door seemed a mystery – although now I can understand it rather better.

The second simplicity

In many ways Clifford Curzon was as daunting and beguiling as Dr Roles and it was probably no accident that they were both Edwardians.

Clifford, I discovered, insisted that the performer's highest achievement was to recover what he called the 'second simplicity'. He explained this very carefully: 'When you first play a piece you can often fully comprehend it immediately. But what is needed then is to go away and take it apart and slowly work your way back to where you can play it just as well as you did the first time but now fully understood. That's what I call the second simplicity.'

Other performers, notably the great singer Janet Baker, have also described the process in very similar terms. We can often immediately grasp things through our emotions and instincts but take much longer to assimilate them using the cognitive 'thinking' mind.

I do not believe that the instinctive and emotional capability of instantly knowing something perfectly 'all at once' is accessible only to musicians. It is a far more common phenomenon than we might sometimes imagine. It is very similar to the experience of falling in love at first sight, which also often carries a similar unquestioned clarity, devoid of caution or indecision.

The only weakness or danger of this immediacy for the performer – and also perhaps for those who fall in love – is that it is vital to work through the thought processes required to sustain the original vision. For musicians this process entails the work of rigorous, analytical rehearsal in order to achieve two things.

Firstly, this type of internal work renders the interpretation stress-proof, so that even in concert the performer can confidently reproduce the quality of his or her original inspiration. Secondly, while retaining the original simplicity, it burnishes the finished performance with a rich patina of unsung possibilities – all the discarded experiments that have been tried out in rehearsal and combine to create a kind of shadowy hinterland of the unrealised. This adds immeasurably to the final interpretation, just as apparently simple words from a wise person carry so much more weight than mere clichés. Dr Roles used to say, 'In order to know the truth you need to know very little, but in order to know that little you need to know pretty much.'

Although only a few key points might need to be *explicitly* retained, Curzon believed that nothing is ever entirely lost from such an exhaustive process of rehearsal and analysis. I have come to share his view that the art of music, as of life, lies not so much in the display of what has been gained but rather in the ability to let go of whatever is not essential to its inner meaning.

Rebuilding my persona after illness has seemed to involve a similar process. What had felt like the defining characteristics of my previous existence now seemed distant, remembered gestures on which a new 'second simplicity' of Self could only gradually be created. This reinvention proved to be surprisingly difficult and took a great deal of time, not least because I discovered that the second time around it needed to be knowingly constructed from a higher set of principles – consciously chosen, rather than the haphazard assembly of often hormonally driven characteristics that congeal together in the formation of a youthful personality.

Irrespective of whether they directly involved music or not, my coma visions seemed to suggest the themes and hitherto unperceived alternatives of my own previous existence – all at once and in their totality. This was like hearing each instrument of an orchestra in perfect detail while remaining fully alive to the emotion of the overall musical architecture.

One vision was particularly precise in its language of alternative lives, Jewishness and food taboos.

A medieval vision

Once again I have become merely one of a number of revolving entities. But this time, instead of a beautiful meditating avatar, the central figure is a pig and the union takes the form of a horrific identification with bestial appetites and farmyard animals.

Some of the action takes place in a small medieval courtyard surrounded by two-storeyed wooden barns that are slightly reminiscent of our current home. The ground is sparsely strewn with scattered hay and the slaughtering of a pig is a key part of the action.

I somehow know this bloody ritual has just occurred, although no actual killing takes place in my presence. I am filled with guilty excitement. There is a disturbing and increasingly uneasy sense of my having relished this bloody event, and I am revolted by my own crude, primitive appetites. This overpowering lust for blood is both repulsive and delicious, and the air seems thick with it. All my senses are strangely alive.

I am aware of myself being a young teenager, full of energy and bursting with excitement. This gory ritual has collapsed my inhibitions and released in their stead a overwhelming craving for blood.

In retrospect, I wonder whether some awareness of the recent bloody assault on my body had released this strange and wild abandon.

The unseen figure of a sacrificial pig clearly offends all Jewish food taboos and could also reference the blood sacrifice in Golding's *Lord of the Flies*, with its disturbing portrayal of humanity stripped of its culture and tumbling into primitive bestiality.

At one level my life has been spent with an almost rabbinical violin imp sitting on one shoulder whispering pious blandishments, while, on the other shoulder, lives his rational counterpart forever pointing out the prejudice and narrow-minded intolerance of conservative Jewish fundamentalism.

Apart from my one and only brief foray into Jewish cultural life at the family wedding and my aunt's absurd bigotry, my only other model of what it might mean to be Jewish was my anxious, superstitious mother. Along with her irrational, neurotic and sporadically extreme vegetarianism, Mum would invariably display genuine panic whenever she thought that I might be at risk of consuming shellfish, pork or skate.

She found even the most secular celebration of Christmas profoundly disturbing. Sadly, in this matter my normally sensible Dad was not a great deal of help. Like any wise and peace-loving husband, rather than tackle Mum's bizarre food fads, he would scrupulously avoid strife by pointing out that in the fishing community of North Shields, where he had been brought up, no one would eat mackerel because of some equally irrational superstition.

Nor could he brighten our appallingly drab and deeply depressing Christmases, which he steadfastly ignored on the grounds that Christmas was a pre-Christian druidic rite adopted and distorted by commercialism and which had no place in the socialist millennium.

So it was that early one Christmas Day I was awoken by our little cat, Tippity, desperately seeking refuge under my bed, pursued by Mum furiously wielding her ancient Hoover. The poor animal actually screamed as Mum repeatedly ran this monstrous roaring machine over her little furry body. I tried not to get involved and desperately hid myself under the covers. When Mum was like this I was just as likely to get run over as the cat.

For lunch that Christmas Day she served us each a single raw turnip. Dad tactfully munched his way through this indigestible offering but, try as I might, I simply couldn't get it down.

Maybe this might explain the peculiar symbolic significance of food and Jewishness that coloured so many of my coma visions. The issue of Jewishness kept recurring, sometimes by the incongruous appearance of Jewish figures, such as Woody Allen, who was in one sequence together with a group of Christmas gnomes, but mostly in a series of food taboos.

One of these sequences involved the awarding of a grand prize for the best steak-and-kidney pie, which, despite its magnificent appearance and smell, nauseated me because of a horrible certainty that the kidney component had come from a pig.

While comatose, the patient is sustained by a carefully balanced nutritious sludge that is funnelled directly into the stomach, and I imagine its meaty smell must have filtered through to me from time to time. During this period I lost many stones in weight and was effectively starving.

I experienced a similar mixture of heady exultation and shame each time I took part in the World Economic Forum at Davos. The thrill of being immersed in a gathering of such untrammelled power and immense wealth was always mixed with a feeling of shame and self-loathing that I should even wish to enter such an amoral playground.

From which we can deduce that my father's ethical influence never left me.

At the end of each visit to Davos I would fall ill. On my final trip I collapsed at the airport and was taken to hospital. Despite numerous tests the doctors could find nothing organically wrong with me. While conscience might express itself psychosomatically, it does not necessarily produce any physical pathology.

Curzon's approach to music-making

Despite his critical and demanding nature it was always clear that, at heart, Clifford's 'afternoon teas' were merely a ritualistic game, while the music-making was deadly serious. Clifford was constantly critical, but he was most critical of himself.

The first work we learned with him was the Dvořák Piano Quintet, which we spent three exasperating weeks preparing. This involved being taken through Clifford's unique rehearsal process, which was exhausting, tiresome and neurotic – but also something I would not have missed for the world.

He began by completely deconstructing the work in a way

reminiscent of how he enjoyed deconstructing me at tea time. We spent hours in the studio with a metronome – but though it was always on, Clifford appeared to make no attempt to play with it. To say the least, this was perplexing.

Playing with a metronome was, of course, familiar to us and we had already spent large parts of our lives doing just that – but this was something entirely different. It didn't help that Clifford seemed blithely unconcerned whether or not we could actually hear his precious metronome. As he had placed it on the music rack of the piano, facing him, we couldn't even see it and were reduced to 'ghosting' along without any chance of matching it.

It soon became clear that Clifford was involved in an entirely personal relationship with the beat. Once the metronome was on he fell into a kind of reverie, wilfully allowing his playing to wander behind or ahead of the beats. Every now and again there would momentarily be an uncanny meeting up of the two and then the wandering began again. We struggled and fretted but Clifford seemed entirely happy, except that now and again he would become irritated with us and tersely demand that we stay with him.

Over the ensuing weeks it gradually dawned on me that Clifford was not even attempting to play with the beat but in fact was 'poeticising' long elaborate phrases while allowing the metronome to act as a record of the underlying rhythmic structure. In other words, instead of observing a strict tempo, he was rehearsing a continually ebbing and flowing expressive rubato that still maintained respect for the beat.

The exasperations of this constant slight variation will be evident, but gradually the rewards began to emerge. Most people who rehearse with a metronome end up sounding as if they have swallowed one and their playing becomes regimented and clunky. Worst of all, such mechanical control destroys any spontaneous flow or natural expressiveness. Slowly and painfully we began to glimpse Clifford's intentions.

I now realise that Clifford's artful teasing of the metronome's rigidity was his expression – as a pianist of inexactitude – of the string players' flexibility of pitch with regard to the Pythagorean gap.

As the performance approached, Clifford was obviously becoming deeply concerned. It was without precedent for him to telephone me at home one evening. Although he did not approach the subject directly he was clearly seeking some kind of acquiescence or rapprochement, asking me a number of times whether I had 'got it' yet.

This felt like a Zen master demanding of his pupil that he must *not* think of a monkey and it obliged me to reconsider both our relationship and our music-making. Most importantly, it made me absolutely intent on standing aside somehow from my own thoughts and assumptions, rather as if he had massaged away a set of 'knots' in my ego.

As we spoke together that evening I felt something inside me suddenly change, as if an inward barrier had been swept away. I confidently assured him we would fulfil his expectations, even though I was still quite unable to articulate or grasp exactly what it was we were talking about.

My interpretation of Clifford's intense behaviour is that such was his developed musical refinement that it could not find expression except through the language of paradox. Over the years I became increasingly fascinated by the phenomenon of paradox, which sets up internal oppositions only in order to reveal the creative space that allows for the resolution of apparently contradictory values.

Shortly after this our violist, Ivo, met Peter Schidlof, the violist of the Amadeus Quartet.

'So. I hear you're playing with Curzon,' Schidlof remarked, and Ivo nodded.

Schidlof raised a quizzical eyebrow.

'That bloody metronome, eh? He keeps it on for hours, doesn't he?'

They both laughed but it was comforting to find we were not alone.

Clifford had the most beautiful and unique piano sound I have ever heard, limpid, utterly pure and sweetly expressive. He would use this to spin endless musical lines, which would arch and feint, then catch again into life and extend on and on . . .

Sadly, this is barely reflected in his many recordings and I suspect that even the finest contemporary recording technology would struggle to capture it. His finesse lay far beyond anything recordable. It seemed to happen somewhere far above your head and in the heart, all at once. The opening chord of the slow movement of the Dvořák Quintet was a particular case in point.

When we were rehearsing he would sit at his piano seemingly involved in something else entirely and then suddenly unloose this exquisitely tender split chord. Irrespective of where I was in the room or what I was doing, every time he did this it was so beautiful that it rendered me strangely weak and unmanned. I would look round and catch him just turning away, a mischievous little grin on his face and, sure enough, a few minutes later, he would do it again.

Sometimes he would play this game all day long and the remarkable feature of this exquisite manipulation was that he was able to repeat it at will. It was a level of mastery I've never encountered since and my recognition of it perhaps explains in part why we became so close.

One day I was leaning over his shoulder in order to read something in the score when I noticed that on the inside front cover he had listed all his previous performances, together with dates and the names of his fellow musicians. First on the list was the original Hungarian Quartet with whom he had played in the year of my birth, 1952. From there on it was a veritable *Who's Who* of all the great post-war European string quartets, including the Budapest, the Léner, the Amadeus, and so on.

Clifford's definitions of artistry

Musicians tend to have their own special qualities, with some being drawn primarily to the beauties of sound while others are fascinated by the structures of music or its relationship to dance and movement and so on.

Putting aside the various personalities involved, there are innate tensions around all musical matters – or are likely to be if the players are intent on facing the inner truths of music.

Clifford insisted that truly great musicians could be recognised by a number of distinctive features. These included having a unique sound, an individual rhythm, and the ability to create moments of complete spontaneity within their performance.

Taking this further I would say that, like great athletes, the finest performers seem to have more time and space for what they do than ordinary mortals usually possess. This means they are able to exercise a much finer degree of discrimination and control over their actions.

I have described something of Clifford's idiosyncratic approach to rhythm. His quality of sound was, if anything, even more developed and remarkable. He once told us how he had sought to introduce his doctor to the secrets of his piano playing.

After inviting the doctor to lay his hands lightly on top of his own while he played, Clifford told him that while anybody could play one note, playing two notes in succession revealed the artist. Clifford's argument was that a performer's whole art could be detected in the 'space between the notes'. He was not alone in this understanding. As Debussy said, 'Music is the space between the notes', and another great pianist, Clifford's teacher Artur Schnabel, commented, 'The notes I handle no better than many pianists. But the pauses between the notes, ah, *that* is where the art resides!'

I am convinced this must be true and it also explains why, in a therapeutic relationship, some people are able to listen quite differently from others and thereby change the emotional space between them. I have met perhaps two psychiatrists with exactly this gift but I have no doubt that many people in other walks of life can also exhibit this precious healing ability.

To see a World in a Grain of Sand
And a Heaven in a Wild Flower,
Hold Infinity in the palm of your hand
And Eternity in an hour.

William Blake

This infinite space between the notes is what we call 'touch' and it is that 'something' that can in a moment lift crude humanity to something almost divine.

Touch

Touch lies at the very heart of the musical experience but remains elusive and difficult to describe.

In his diverting book *The Third Policeman*, Flann O'Brien found a wonderfully original way of illuminating the otherwise indescribable through deliciously absurd paradoxes. Over many years the titular policeman and his bicycle have exchanged so many molecules that they have also begun to swap identities. The policeman can usually be found propped up against the bar of the local pub while his bicycle shows up unexpectedly around the village without him.

In popular culture violinists have become interchangeable with their voluptuous instruments – alluringly sensual, strangely sexually ambivalent, much given to 'stirring the blood'. Remember Tolstoy's violently erotic novella, *The Kreutzer Sonata*? Violinists are often portrayed as mysterious and frightening manifestations, including the devil himself, who is frequently pictured playing the violin. Not to mention Tartini's 'Devil's Trill' Sonata or Paganini's supposedly fiendish virtuosity.

Violinists typically hibernate during daylight, presumably like their violins, in velvet-lined coffins, emerging only at night to gorge on the blood of their helplessly impressionable victims. That the playing position of the early viols gradually migrated up to the nerve ganglions of the neck suggests a journey towards this quasi-erotic source of sustenance.

Dangerous 'outsiders'– such as Jews or gypsies and violinists – are imagined practising arcane magical arts so that
'respectable' people are drawn to them as if to a hallucinatory
drug. Those drawn by some imperative to this 'dark' side
include such drug-takers as Sherlock Holmes, shamans and
other purveyors of the miraculous.

Another of O'Brien's charming metaphors is a needle so
sharp that its point can neither be seen nor felt, and a unique
piece of material whose colour and texture, once perceived,
can be neither forgotten nor described. Contact with these
'impossible' objects commonly sends people mad. So, in
O'Brien's story, they are kept under lock and key.

'Touch' shares similar magic properties. At its most refined
it is virtually imperceptible. Its effect is observed the night
before the battle of Agincourt by the Chorus in Shakespeare's
Henry V:

> *Nor doth he dedicate one jot of colour*
> *Unto the weary and all-watched night;*
> *But freshly looks, and over-bears attaint*
> *With cheerful semblance and sweet majesty;*
> *That every wretch, pining and pale before,*
> *Beholding him, plucks comfort from his looks;*
> *A largess universal, like the sun,*
> *His liberal eye doth give to every one,*
> *Thawing cold fear, that mean and gentle all*
> *Behold, as may unworthiness define,*
> *A little* touch *of Harry in the night.*

To the performer 'touch' is closely related to what psychologists describe as 'locus of control'. Inspiration can be forthcoming from outside or inside: some higher self or the hidden depths of our unconscious. The recognition of a performer's inspired touch seems to connect us instantly to some wondrous divinity.

We speak of a touch of class, genius or inspiration. We can conceive of a healing or magical touch, as we can understand what is meant by being touched up. If we lose control and are no longer in command of our feelings, we may be thought to be touched by madness or by a different kind of genius. Plato believed that the inspired artist is rendered effectively 'mindless' – what we might now consider as no longer 'being of sound mind'.

Music literally touches us with the molecular energy of sound, and all great players exhibit a special, individual quality of touch on their instruments. In the context of instrumental performance, touch is also intimately bound up with tone and pulse: the 'life force' of all that is creative.

Tone is also our psychological measure of all kinds of subtle values, including our moral tone, emotional tone and general state, as when we are well toned or attuned. Our rhythmic pulse is inextricably linked with our heart (both anatomically and figuratively) and our breathing – in fact our whole autonomic nervous system, which is the physical seat of our spiritual life, experience and capability.

Each of these interconnected systems can be mediated, developed and directed by our level of attention, and of course through the quality and rhythm of our breathing. Here then is the complex of profound qualities that constitute our 'being', each and all of which is conveyed through touch. Touch reveals everything about us.

When the sensitivity of touch is sufficiently highly developed – as when it responds to O'Brien's exquisite needle – it can extend into the intangible field of energy that lies between and beyond individuals. We may call this ESP, or prayer, or love, or the Divine, or the space between the notes – or whatever else we will. Leonardo's miraculous Sistine Chapel depiction of God creating Adam captures exactly this profound and beautiful mystery. The energy that passes between the Maker and his creation is precisely that between the violinist and his instrument, the performer and his audience, the quartet player and his colleagues, and so on.

For the purposes of this book, at least, this is the ineffable 'stuff' of music.

Learning Elgar with Clifford

After we had been playing together for a couple of years I discovered that Clifford didn't know the Elgar Piano Quintet, despite its significant place in the composer's output. I therefore proposed to him that we learn the work together. Rather taken aback, he considered this idea and to my delight some weeks later announced that he was willing to add this piece to his repertoire. I was thrilled, but only dimly conceived what a coup it was to receive such a concession from this elderly maestro.

His preparation was highly individualistic and deeply personal and, thank God, he made it a condition that I participate in the whole of it. Firstly, he bought a copy of the score, which he did not open until he had thoroughly studied Elgar's life, personality and psychology. Only after all this did he begin to study the actual music.

One afternoon I was summoned by Clifford to drive into the quintessential English countryside to visit Brinkwells near Fittleworth. Sitting together, we listened to the very first recording of the Piano Quintet recorded on old 78 rpm discs.

Shortly after the music began, Clifford leant forward in his chair and tapped me on the knee. For two typically inhibited Englishmen of the era, such physical contact was as shocking as Clifford clearly meant it to be.

'Remember this moment, Paul,' he said, 'Music sounds quite different when you listen to it in the presence of a master.' This was not said with pride but simply as an important observation. Of course he was right and I never forgot it, nor the powerful impression the music made on me.

Another day we drove together all the way to Elgar's Birthplace Museum in Malvern where the curator, awed by Clifford's presence, instantly volunteered to open the case holding Elgar's personal possessions. These included the autograph manuscript of the Piano Quintet and the violin Elgar had played as a child prodigy.

Clifford took time to hold and examine each of the exhibits very carefully, handling them almost reverentially, quietly insisting that I should do so too.

He also observed exactly how the ink from Elgar's pen had marked the paper. He admitted that for the last few weeks he had been sleeping with the unopened score of the Piano Quintet under his pillow. Although no one would seriously suggest that this could convey its musical secrets, this delicate confidence did allow me to see the value of liberating the imagination.

Without such enriched 'imagination' music is doomed to remain dull and pedestrian, as is so much of life. Any suggestion that the imaginative is not real or true would be quite wrong. Imagination might not yield many facts but it can reveal the 'truth' about reality because whatever we believe to be real is entirely a matter of interpretation. Even if we cannot bring ourselves to acknowledge an imaginative Deity we can observe how Nature is wonderfully florid, exaggerated and deliciously flamboyant. It is hardly an original idea to suggest that Nature is God's imagination in full flow.

This visit to the Malvern Hills made a huge impression on me and elements of it arose in a number of my coma visions.

In one of them, I experienced a lingering sojourn in a home for wounded officers located somewhere in Shropshire (Malvern is actually in Worcestershire) with its reminiscences of Housman's and Wilfred Owen's poetry, Vaughan Williams's haunting 'On Wenlock Edge', Butterworth's 'Shropshire Lad' settings, Siegfried Sassoon's autobiography and, perhaps above all, Edward Elgar.

In Shropshire

I am about thirty years old and find myself in a quiet and spacious Edwardian or Victorian convalescent home situated somewhere deep in the Shropshire countryside.

I feel ill and weak and presume myself to be either recovering from or perhaps succumbing to tuberculosis or a war wound. I am not in uniform but there is somehow a very old-fashioned and gentlemanly graciousness about the style and habits of this place.

Although I do not see them, figures such as Elgar, Kipling, Herbert Howells and other Edwardian artists are all somehow associated with this quintessentially 'English' place. From time to time I am aware of hearing a distant cuckoo calling.

This cuckoo has special significance as it is the only non-Indian sound I remember hearing during all these coma visions.

And, thinking back to my childhood singing lesson, the distinctive call of the cuckoo was also my personal gateway into the world of music.

The Cuckoo remembered

This particular dream sequence had many associations with Siegfried Sassoon's autobiography, *Memoirs of a Fox-Hunting Man*. It is a book that fascinated me at one period, not least because Sassoon writes so acutely about a vacuous life that gradually becomes full of depth. Somehow Sassoon achieves this without the least bombast or fuss. He was a much decorated war hero, and subsequently won unusual renown by being the only British officer openly to criticise the conduct of the First World War while it was still being fought. At that time only someone so eminent and courageous could possibly have got away with public statements of that kind without facing a court-martial and risking a firing squad for cowardice or treason.

He was committed into the care of Dr William Rivers, the fine and groundbreaking psychiatrist who first identified and began to treat 'shell shock', which is now fully accepted as post-traumatic stress disorder (PTSD). To my mind, Sassoon's conscientious stand brought him into an honourable alignment with my father's principled pacifism.

Another aspect of Sassoon's personal life that could not be openly acknowledged at the time was his homosexuality.

The pervading Edwardian fustiness and gentle charm of this vast 'remembered' house and its bucolic setting were altogether reminiscent of my time learning the Elgar Piano Quintet with Clifford Curzon, demonstrating again how the imagery of these coma 'memories' was so richly layered and how deeply Edwardian some part of my psyche must be.

If we are to consider that any of these vivid dreams are in some way actual remembered experiences, I would have to say that I *was* a junior officer in the First World War.

For Clifford, learning the Elgar meant revisiting of his own childhood. His earliest musical memory was of creeping out of bed onto the landing and listening to his famous brother-in-law, the composer Albert Ketèlbey, playing the piano downstairs. Ketèlbey was the composer of numerous popular, light-classical Edwardian pieces such as 'In a Monastery Garden'.

Children naturally feel drawn to their grandparents' memories because they connect them to the furthest time in the past that remains alive. As Norbert Brainin, the leader of the Amadeus Quartet, pointed out when we went to him for coaching on my favourite Schubert quartet, the A minor (D. 804), 'I feel sorry for your generation trying to play Schubert because you are one whole generation further away from the composer – that, and you can never experience the unique sound of pre-motor car Vienna.'

Places in particular eras are infused with unique timbres and soundscapes for musicians, just as they generate specific colours and hues for visual artists.

Curzon's journey into Elgar's musical world

One morning while we were learning the Elgar, Curzon, still putting in his cufflinks, opened the door to me in high excitement. Hastily ushering me in, he announced he had at last decoded Elgar's musical impulse. He said that Elgar had harboured a lifelong inferiority complex because his father had been a mere piano-tuner. The sensitive young Elgar had grown to loathe the piano because after his father had tuned the instruments he obliged his son to perform on them for the owners, a task he had found deeply demeaning. Discovering all this had convinced Clifford that the Piano Quintet, Elgar's only major work for the piano, includes passages distinctly reminiscent of a tuner strumming spread chords on the keyboard after it has been tuned – and that these could clearly be heard in certain passages of the slow movement. As Elgar's last significant composition this also made it a personal testament and a valediction of his childhood, his lifelong feelings of inadequacy and of being a scorned Catholic in a provincial Protestant society. This was not all. His clinching insight was a triumphant announcement, 'Of course Elgar masturbated at the piano!' Having now revealed these psychological insights, Clifford set about learning and playing the work with exceptional zeal and sensitivity.

Sadly, we performed the Quintet with him only once, but it remains one of the musical highlights of my life: erotic and transforming. During the performance I recall glancing across to him during the almost endless ecstatic climax of the slow movement and recognising that as he was negotiating the musical architecture he was possessed by a kind of sexual haze, as was I.

This was the first time that I explicitly understood how close and exalted the connection is between music and sexual love.

Although Clifford's Freudian analysis cannot be proved one way or the other, I invite anyone to listen to the fascinating piano improvisations that Elgar insisted on recording towards the end of his life. When Clifford discovered these very personal musical statements he demanded I listen to them, for he felt they not only revealed Elgar's essential musical spirit but also pointed to a rather naive eroticism. Perhaps all arousal states are similar in structure; certainly many works of 'high' art suggest having their roots deep within very personal erotic impulses.

Whatever the truth or otherwise of Clifford's insights I never doubted their validity for him, and the subtle authority of his interpretations was masterful and unique. His personal inner language of symbol and metaphor allowed him a powerful intimacy with the music, which was made sublime by his elevated aesthetic sensibilities. His tender, pellucid tone and infinitely subtle melodic musical lines were simply unsurpassed.

Postscript

When I was young there was a popular little joke about the Builders' Association attempt on Everest, which failed when they ran out of scaffolding at 10,000 feet. Trying to describe 'higher' emotional or spiritual states often falters and fails because of a similarly absurd assumption. It is impossible to encompass or comprehend the exalted by means of the material.

Spirituality, consciousness and music all belong to a category of experience in which the whole is greater than the sum of its parts. For this reason I cannot accept the current rationalist assumption that human consciousness is merely incidental to our cognitive intelligence or that our musical experience is the accidental result of a fortuitous combination of otherwise unconnected evolutionary gifts.

Serious science demands and deserves the most critical assessment of verifiable facts, just as a musical performance demands diligence in playing the right notes, in the correct order and at the right tempo. But neither fact nor accuracy adds up to meaning – and even though musical forms can be reduced to mathematical algorithms, even the most brilliant computer programs have, to date, been unable to generate anything like the wonders of J. S. Bach, whose works are so much more than just mathematical ciphers.

Conscious design is not a matter of chance, and consciousness itself cannot be created mechanically. A billion monkeys hitting typewriters will never *create* Shakespeare although they might accidentally reproduce the words. Neither is art 'sublimated sex', even though much artistic expression is motivated by a divinely inspired urge to create.

At every turn, inspiration supersedes diligence just as intention overtakes chance, although each one of these has its place in the creative order.

The heightened emotional communication that music and love can release is essentially the same consciously creative energy that shapes and evolves life itself. Unsurprisingly, at the point of death, this life energy is released so that we leave this mortal realm comprehending that all our previous 'letting go' has been only a rehearsal for what we really need on our onward journey. And what follows then? I hope and believe it is a return to that 'second simplicity', which lies in the space between lives – just as music lives between the notes.

Why do we cling to life?

My experience as I 'died' was that I had no wish to carry anything with me and was gladly able to shed my superficial ego and individual personality in order to travel beyond the threshold of myself into the transcendent, eternal beauty of the universe. At this precious moment the longing to join this Infinity was so powerful that I suddenly saw all my familiar psychological apparel merely as an old suit of clothes that could gladly be abandoned.

But if the next life is so appealing, why do we cling so desperately to this earthly existence? And if the sight of eternity is as glorious as I suggest, why would anyone choose to return? These seem entirely natural questions, which I continue to ask myself.

A fear of dying is clearly a necessary part of our material existence for without it we might never fulfil our biological obligation to ensure the future of the species. This might also explain why most of us arrive in the world without any lucid memories or certain knowledge of the Infinity that surrounds us. After all, there must be compelling reasons why some individuals who are already in paradise elect to return to life.

Sometimes, people report that their loved ones call them back and they return out of love for others, and this might have been partially true for me. Another powerful motive can be when we feel there is vital unfinished business that can be dealt with only in the here and now of physical existence. Only while we are physically alive can we experience free will and choice – in other words those key powers that seem to render human experience uniquely meaningful. It became absolutely clear to me that no significant personal or emotional change is possible once we merge back into the Infinite – because from then on we no longer possess any individual independent existence.

Much of the consolation of becoming freed from life was that all decision-making was lifted from me and I found this sensation of complete freedom wonderfully liberating.

So, as we leave life, who or what is it that 'elects' whether we should live or die?

While I was actually 'dead' I had no choice whatever – because at that point I no longer existed, but the visions and hallucinations that I experienced as I lay on the trembling cusp of consciousness and existence acted as faint echoes of my moral self. This convinces me that human life at its deepest level is not entirely defined by any physical or material embodiment, but is primarily endowed as a *moral* force.

Even though I was not at all aware of myself while in coma, once I returned to life I never doubted that it was 'my' decision to have chosen to live. What might this mean and how can it happen?

This is possible because the universe is itself imbued with consciousness and that 'pure consciousness' is its ultimate nature. Even though we might not always appreciate it, such a numinous consciousness always recognises and upholds what is right and what is true.

In other words, this cosmic force has much in common with our impulse to follow our 'conscience' because the same underlying principle is reflected in both. Conscience and consciousness are two sides of the same coin and I believe that the 'moral' visions of my comas were consciousness being presented in its elemental form.

As my other mentor, Dr Roles, used to say: 'At the human level "consciousness" means *knowing* the truth all at once while "conscience" means *feeling* the truth all at once. In the midst of life it is the emotional power of conscience, as an individual, moral perception, that provides the key to open our perception to the infinite light of pure consciousness. Conscience is the pure voice of truth that speaks to us through the door of the heart – as long as we consciously hold that door open.'

While I was 'dead', only the greater, pure consciousness was present, but once my personal identity flicked back into play this greater consciousness was channelled once again through the filter of my own much more limited understanding. Throughout the universe, just as in ourselves, there is always a moral consciousness at work; one level reflects an all-knowing consciousness and the other expresses that smaller part we call 'I'. That's the way it is.

Altered perception

In the intensive care unit I continued to be very seriously ill and I was often delirious. While hovering in this limbo between two worlds, my perspectives became strange and spectral. I was primarily aware of those around me only as spiritual entities whose auras were entirely transparent. Within this mode of perception many of the nurses seemed barely sentient and one or two of them disturbed me deeply as their apparent indifference bordered on the malign. Two of the nurses, however, stood out as 'angelic'.

One of them was unusually devout. Although I was far too ill to see her clearly, I could sense the force of her faith. Curiously enough, she seemed to have the same first name as my wife: Chika. I felt that although she accepted that the outcome of my illness (as with everyone else's) was in the hands of God, she would be tireless in her devotion to help me survive. I later found that this nurse, whose name was indeed Chika, had confidently told my wife that I was destined to recover in order to write a book. She even went so far as to volunteer to help me write it.

The other 'angelic' nurse struck me as someone genuinely divinely inspired. Even when she was out of my field of vision, I always sensed immediately she entered the ward. She would stand compassionately by each patient in turn, love pouring from her like a golden light. I longed for her to reach me, when even the lightest touch of her fingers as she straightened the bedclothes was a benediction.

I now wonder if I was perceiving her compassion as beauty. But this is now the way I see everyone. Some people may be superficially attractive, but true beauty is lit up from within by spiritual empathy and love. Such a divine, healing touch is the property of another, miraculous world that can be conveyed into our own only through the transparency and insight of love.

In sharing these experiences I am not suggesting that they should necessarily be taken as representative of universal truth. Human beings have a remarkable capacity to create symbols out of perception, and interpret life in much the same way as we interpret music: uncertainly, personally, with our judgement coloured by all the idiosyncrasies and accumulations of our own histories and cultures. Whatever we deem 'real' or 'true' about human experience is inevitably and unavoidably a function of an accumulation of subjective interpretation and faith.

The wonder of it is that we can still catch a glimpse of heaven, even, as it were, 'through a glass, darkly'. I cannot claim that my interpretation is inherently more truthful than anyone else's. But as the recipient and 'progenitor' of my own imagery, I have a privileged insight into my own experience.

I am propelled to Gurdjieff

Now to introduce the other great spiritual guide of my life: Dr Francis Roles.

I came into contact with this remarkable man through a series of curious synchronicities that I would now accept as 'divine'.

During my early twenties, full of questions, I found myself increasingly drawn to the extensive psychology section of Blackwell's vast bookshop in Oxford. At that time, the psychology and philosophy departments were housed in the basement.

Wandering aimlessly into the shop one day I was descending the stairs when someone shoved me hard between my shoulder blades. Stumbling down the last two or three steps I sprawled across the floor, instinctively raising my right arm in order to break my fall. As I looked up, I saw that my hand had come to rest on a strange and exotic little book. I felt instantly drawn to it, but before pulling it out I looked around to see who had pushed me down the stairs. There was no one there.

The book had a curious title, *Beelzebub's Tales to his Grandson*, and was the first in a set of three. The author was G. I. Gurdjieff, of whom I had never heard. I bought all three volumes, and spent a year trying to read them. They were dense, bizarre and largely incomprehensible.

Yet, as I persisted, I could feel my interior life being shunted around inside me like furniture in a house and by the time I had finished the books I was in a state of complete confusion. I sensed that the author had many answers and even better questions, but I found it impossible to understand most of what he had written. All this combined to make me deeply dissatisfied and frustrated with my habits of thought and manner of living.

Several months later I awoke one morning with a strange feeling in my lower back and an awareness that I had just been told, in a dream, that my soul felt 'dirty'. This was completely unexpected, for my upbringing made no allowance for any concept of a soul, still less of a God. My parents scorned all forms of religious observance and at the time I largely shared their scepticism, although I lacked their radical zeal.

All this finally led me to seek out a local GP, Dr Michael Cox, who practised as a medical homeopath. We had a long and engaged conversation, and finally I referred to Gurdjieff's book and my problems understanding it. At the mention of this name he suddenly looked up at me with renewed interest and recommended I contact a society he knew of, as it was 'impossible to comprehend Gurdjieff without guidance'. He gave me a phone number to call and suggested I make an appointment.

This turned out to be the Study Society and thus the deep and formative influence I found in Dr Roles was set in train. It was only long afterwards that it struck me how remarkable it was that our paths had crossed in this way and that he should already be so familiar with this strange writer.

Being pushed down the stairs by invisible hands is not a common experience for most of us and I have only twice known people who reported such incidents in their lives. When he was three years old our son began shouting angrily at a chair in the garden insisting it had 'thrown him off'. From where I was sitting it looked much more as if he had simply miscalculated the force of gravity, but all that day he insisted this was not the case. Never before or since has he expressed such anger.

Years later, when my mother was dying and very frail, one night she fell and broke her hip. She was absolutely insistent that someone had knocked her down, although we knew that the other members of the family were all tucked up in their own beds at the time. Even though she seemed not to realise just how physically damaged she was following this accident, she definitely sensed the event as having been somehow malign and personal.

In the hands of fate

I have occasionally heard accounts of people who claim to have been guided by unseen hands but I have always assumed such stories to be the product of an over-active imagination. If they seemed sincere, I put their conviction down to some kind of self-induced hysterical manifestation. I would be content to include my own story in this category were it not for the fact that it led me to the discovery of such a significant and lastingly influential psychological thread in my life. To me, this whole episode smacks of an external conscious agency so much so that I now openly acknowledge these implications.

I should also mention that at the Study Society, for perfectly sound and rational reasons, Gurdjieff's own line of teaching was never referred to. However, because of my personal history, I could never fully accept this restriction. I still believe that in some sense it was Gurdjieff's personal spirit that directed my auspicious fall in that Oxford bookshop.

Incidents of the sort I describe become more easily explicable once our perception is suitably primed – and music provides many of us with exactly such an emotional priming. It could well be that the world becomes a very different place for musicians and others who function regularly in this way.

Fortunately for most of us these 'altered states' do not require that we be at death's door, though many of them demand that we 'let go' of ourselves in some way.

When I first knew him, Dr Roles was the head of a very private 'esoteric school' that taught and followed various ancient traditions and teachings, including a particular form of transcendental meditation.

This organisation was called the Society for the Study of Normal Psychology (usually known as the Study Society) and its meetings took place in a very grand and rather wonderful house at Barons Court in West London. This building, Colet House, had once belonged to a fashionable Victorian painter and later served as the home of Diaghilev's Ballets Russes company before becoming the London centre for the teachings of the Russian philosopher and writer P. D. Ouspensky. Ouspensky himself had been a pupil of the mystic George Gurdjieff, before establishing his own separate line of teaching.

To start with I was placed in the Beginners' Group, which was designed to introduce the basic principles of the Work and in particular the arcane System of the ancient Enneagram. The weekly meetings of this group were taken by one of Ouspensky's pupils, Professor Richard Guyatt, whom I came to revere as a man of exceptional dedication and rare discriminating intelligence. For the first two years I pestered and harassed this wonderful man with a veritable barrage of challenging, sceptical and often downright rude questions.

Each successive week he would respond to my previous week's questions with care and fastidious seriousness, always making it clear that each response had been shaped in consultation with the head of the school, namely, Dr Francis Roles.

After nearly three years of cross-examination I decided it was time to see this Dr Roles in action and finally attended one of the doctor's big Sunday meetings.

As soon as he entered I knew this was a man of exceptional quality. He was quiet, still, authoritative and utterly controlled. It was the first time I ever saw such qualities away from a musical instrument and I was deeply impressed.

I learned that some years after Ouspensky's death and in accordance with his dying wishes, Dr Roles had eventually succeeded in identifying, as one of the original sources of both Ouspensky's and Gurdjieff's teaching, the ancient Indian Shankaracharya tradition of Advaita non-dualism with its special form of meditation. Since then, and until his death in 1982, he had maintained a remarkable direct relationship with the then incumbent, Swami Shantananda Saraswati.

Dr Roles held personal conversations and prepared for his meetings in a special room that had been Ouspensky's private study at Colet House, a most elegant inner sanctum with a particularly tranquil yet powerful atmosphere. Like his teacher, Ouspensky, Dr Roles had that rarest of qualities: he loved the Truth, at any cost.

These relationships were developing as I was beginning to work with my other key mentor, the pianist Sir Clifford Curzon. During this same period I also fell suddenly and desperately in love. Before marrying, I felt I should take advice and so arranged to go and see Dr Roles at his home at Waterton House on the banks of the River Thames in Twickenham.

Towards the end of his life, Dr Roles was rather deaf and at the time of this meeting his wife of more than fifty years was approaching death in her bedroom upstairs. He finally heard me ringing the bell and ushered me in, sat me down and asked kindly what he could do for me. I explained that I wanted him to answer a question that I was not going to ask him.

For a brief moment he looked furious. I always sensed he had a fierce temper, though he seldom expressed it and never without purpose. Then he looked very keenly at me and smiled. In fact he almost laughed.

'But am I at least allowed to ask *you* questions?'

'Of course,' I replied.

He looked delighted. 'So this is a kind of test?' he asked.

'Absolutely!'

We then proceeded to have a delightful and wide-ranging conversation during which I told him all about my burgeoning string quartet and musical ambitions. Although I was not aware of it, as a skilled physician he was of course collating all this in order to make a 'diagnosis' of my unasked question. He referred to his deafness and spoke about his wife and then asked about my feelings towards the Study Society.

Finally he said, 'So what you want to know is whether it is all right for you to marry and whether it is a good decision.' Hurray! We had arrived.

I explained that I felt it had taken more than one lifetime for me to reach the School and that I had a deadly fear that my new wife might not understand or approve. What would I do if this happened?

He proceeded to give me all sorts of really good practical advice. Firstly, he made it clear that my first obligation was to my wife. 'You must remember she may well have her own traditions and spiritual practice and you must respect that.' He also briefly described some of the miseries and difficulties that arose when couples could not come to an agreement about School work.

He said he believed I had everything I needed to become a 'complete' person but that I also had an almighty ego, which I would have to learn to let go of if I was to move forward. He then asked about my sex life – not in any unhealthy way but just as a doctor might.

I enthused, and then he said, 'You know, there is a huge difference between your generation and mine.' As he spoke he pointed to his neck. 'When I was your age we simply didn't think women existed from here downwards.' Then, with his hand still indicating his neck, he continued, 'Now, you don't even consider women exist from there upwards.' Of course he was right, but as he spoke I thought I caught a slightly wistful look in his eye.

Just before we parted company on this occasion, I asked him whether he thought that in time I would be capable of achieving Self-realisation. He looked at me with a wry expression and said again that he felt I had 'everything necessary to do this but really would have to learn what it meant to lose my over-developed ego'.

Like the disciple in the Hindu story, whose teacher promises him enlightenment after the same number of years have passed as there are leaves on the banyan tree he is sitting under, I was delighted by this answer. Who cares how long something takes? That's what we are alive to do.

The symbolism of this next coma vision references Dr Roles and the Study Society, but most significantly it conveys the importance of letting the ego 'die' in order to discover a greater insight. This is the account of the episode as I originally wrote it, following my initial recovery.

In an Indian shrine

I am in a spiritual centre, an ashram, somewhere in India. Although I am highly regarded in this place, it is required that I allow myself to be bitten by a small but potentially deadly snake. It bites me in the arm (presumably this was a reaction to an injection) and it seems uncertain whether I will survive this ordeal. The retreat is very beautiful and everyone moves gracefully and quietly. However, it is also stifling and airless, and I am unpleasantly feverish and find it hard to breathe freely. (Dr Roles suffered from emphysema at the end of his life.) Although I am much concerned about my own mortality and greatly troubled by the stifling heat of India, no one else seems remotely concerned. Once again there is a wonderfully exotic woman's voice singing consoling *bhajan*s somewhere in the background.

I feel strangely alone and distant even when there is another person in the room. I am certain that this was Dr Roles's inner sanctum. The vision also seems to anticipate my current thoughts about the nature of 'divine sacrifice'.

This was by no means the end of this exceptional man's lasting influence on me, but over the years, thinking about my 'test' of Dr Roles, I realised that what he had brilliantly demonstrated was a fine, empathetic, inductive and intuitive intelligence at work, of the sort one always hopes to find in a GP but in fact so rarely does.

As time went by I began to discover similar abilities within myself, although most of them were naturally exercised musically rather than medically. Nowadays, I recognise that all human beings share the capacity to develop and use such gifts because they are hard-wired into all of us as the highly developed social mammals we are. It is probably because of this universal ability that we make and use music, which is one of nature's best-endowed playgrounds of non-verbal communication.

This congruence of intuition and calculation could also account for the close association between music and medicine.

My own empathic qualities (which were to be massively distorted by a selfishness born of insecurity and a chronic lack of trust) first showed up with the violin, but they were also very much a part of my early emotional life – as I am sure they are for most young humans.

> *Lift not the painted veil which those who live*
> *Call Life: though unreal shapes be pictured there . . .*
> Percy Bysshe Shelley

C. S. Lewis's children's books about the magical realm of Narnia shaped much of my childhood. Exploring as they do the philosophical nature of Christian mysticism, Lewis suggests that there are places where the separation between this world and others is thinner or more permeable than normal.

According to him these different worlds each lie close by, side by side, ready to become apparent as soon as our perceptual system lowers its guard, and it might well be that each of us constantly unwittingly slides between these worlds (or different levels of consciousness), remaining largely unaware that we are doing it.

Between these worlds are nodal points, which Lewis symbolically described as a non-located timeless place.

In ancient mythology this space between worlds was commonly described as a river or ocean, such as the Styx or Oceanus; we find it still in Christian baptism and other rites of passage.

What is certain is that irrespective of its social form or spiritual metaphor, music provides us with precisely such an internal nexus for spiritual travel and transcendence.

Understood in these terms, musicians must be – and are – our cultural shamans.

I hear an internal voice

Like many other imaginative people, at moments of crisis I have occasionally 'heard' an authoritative internal voice directing me. I have also been through the torrid business of choosing not to obey this voice when I concluded it was directing me against my conscience.

Despite the comfort such internally evoked voices can provide, I have always assumed that they were unconsciously self-induced in order to express otherwise unheeded needs or desires. But on just one occasion I 'heard' an internal voice of an entirely different nature.

This took place at one of the weekly meetings at the Study Society, presided over by Dr Roles, and these lovely meetings would usually end with a meditation. At the end of one such meeting, as I was sitting, eyes shut and quietly meditating, I suddenly felt something bizarre yet beautiful. I distinctly heard and felt the doctor's voice 'speaking' directly in my heart and chest. It was clearly him and it is impossible to describe in any other way, but for a short while I felt his voice resonating within me, almost as if my diaphragm was acting as a loudspeaker. I was so shocked that I opened my eyes to find myself looking directly into the eyes of the doctor, who was sitting on the podium and staring intently at me.

As the meeting came to a close I felt confused and dazed. The doctor, then in his late seventies, walked slowly down the room, stood next to me and pressed the knuckles of his hand firmly into my chest, in exactly the place where I had felt his voice. He then proceeded to push and turn his knuckles uncomfortably into this same spot. The sheer physicality of this action registered the experience as a deeply somatic memory, so literally 'embodied' that I could not possibly deny it to myself afterwards.

Was this miraculous or merely an extreme example of imagination and empathy? In either case I think a simple 'yes' will suffice. My only regret is that I cannot now recall precisely what it was that the doctor conveyed to me in the words I heard from him. However, I am utterly certain that they will resurface with complete clarity whenever they are needed.

I discovered later that P. D. Ouspensky recorded a remarkably similar experience that he had with his teacher, Gurdjieff, in the book *In Search of the Miraculous*.

I compathise Oistrakh's vibrato

Along with sympathy and empathy, the medical fraternity sometimes speaks of 'compathy'. Sympathy is feeling *for* someone and empathy *with* them, but compathy describes people (often carers) who find themselves actually feeling exactly the same physical symptoms as their patient. For obvious therapeutic reasons this is not encouraged and can even become comedic in extreme cases, such as when young fathers-to-be display the symptoms of pregnancy and labour. However, I am sure that it is just this human capacity that allows us to experience some types of ESP.

When I was twenty-one, the greatest violinist of his time, David Oistrakh, died. I remember it vividly. I was at home watching television when the news was announced. As part of its tribute, the BBC showed a brief clip of him as a young man winning the Tchaikovsky Violin Competition. I was instantly spellbound. At that time, although already a good player, I had a particularly wide and slow vibrato.

In some respects this generous vibrato was my saving grace, as it allowed my left hand to remain relaxed and free from the repetitive strain injuries that can beset aspiring young players – but the result was a rather wobbly tone. The little finger vibrato is particularly tricky for nominally the weakest and least independent digit.

Oistrakh had a wonderful vibrato, at once emotional yet entirely natural, and in the few seconds he was on the screen I suddenly saw exactly how he was achieving this glorious effect, even with his little finger.

Oistrakh's technique was somewhat contentious in the violin world since his habit of lifting his left-hand fingers unnecessarily is generally considered bad practice as it tends to makes the hand slower and less proficient. I observed that as soon as he brought his little finger into play he was instantly able to 'connect' it up through his hand and thence into his arm.

His arm remained unusually loose and freely connected into the arm socket from where it directly expressed his emotional imagination. Even his 'place of direction' became clear to me, which was evidently focused, like a third eye, in the middle of his forehead.

In this way I realised that Oistrakh's playing was entirely a matter of intention and imagination. All this I saw and comprehended in a split second and I remember running out of the room shouting that 'now I understand'.

From that time onwards I enjoyed an excellent vibrato, which remained intact as long as I did not try to over-direct it. So much for 'imitation'.

All these fine men who influenced me in their various ways were themselves content to be obedient disciples, respectfully following others within their own distinguished traditions. To my surprise I could not find anything mindlessly 'slavish' or unquestioningly conventional in any of them – quite the contrary in fact.

This must have created a significant inner turmoil within me as it did not sit comfortably with my radical socialist upbringing. I rather suspect that some of these dilemmas found expression in this next coma hallucination. Even Clifford's qualities and anachronistic observance of Edwardian tea drinking found resonance and symbolic expression in this particular coma vision.

In this, my most 'quiet' vision, I am an old Japanese lady in a retirement home. Slowly and carefully I am trying to prepare a low circular table in order to celebrate one final tea with my children and grandchildren. I am hoping so much that they are on their way and I can live long enough to see them and drink tea with them.

I feel so exhausted and frail that while appreciating the ceremony of serving tea, I am completely uninterested in drinking it. I know that in my past the delicate porcelain tea set has seemed very precious but now I feel so tired I no longer care. I am able to move only slowly and with difficulty, and my breathing is laboured. I sense this is probably the very last tea I can arrange for my family and I shall then take to my bed and die.

While this might be some kind of 'past life' memory or perhaps an anticipation of a life not yet lived, it is also a rather clever combination of my affection for my Japanese wife's family, with their underlying restraint and tradition, and my great fondness for Clifford Curzon and the precious time we spent together.

It was during my time with Clifford that Chika and I met and married. My wedding ring had been her father's, and although I never knew him (he died when she was nineteen), I still often feel his benign presence when wearing it.

Beethoven

*Until one is committed, there is hesitancy, the chance to draw
back, always ineffectiveness. Concerning all acts of initiative
and creation, there is one elementary truth the ignorance
of which kills countless ideas and splendid plans: that the
moment one definitely commits oneself, then providence moves
too. A whole stream of events issues from the decision, raising
in one's favour all manner of unforeseen incidents, meetings
and material assistance, which no man could have dreamt
would have come his way.*

W. H. Murray, *The Scottish Himalaya Expedition* (inspired by a free
translation of Goethe by John Anster)

We commit our personalities to Beethoven

One afternoon before a rehearsal, our cellist Lew mentioned
that he'd just had an interesting conversation with a neighbour he'd bumped into at the pub.

'Apparently this chap's what they call a *management consultant*,' he told us excitedly.

'And what's that when it's at home?' someone else enquired.
I was also mildly intrigued as I'd never heard of such people
either.

'Well, I didn't really understand it much, but apparently he
goes into companies and things and tells them what to do,' he
said vaguely.

'Yes, but what kind of things?' I demanded to know. Lew
looked a bit disconcerted but attempted to explain.

'Well, apparently in organisations and businesses they

sometimes get together and discuss things like – like, where they want to go and how they're going to get there.'

I recall laughing out loud at this. How stupid! Of course we knew exactly where we were going. We were going where I said we were. But before I could say this I noticed that my colleagues were all clearly engaged by this novel idea and were already discussing it animatedly.

This was uncharacteristic, so I observed with interest where it might lead. After a short while I became bored with their lack of progress and took charge in my usual fashion. 'Since you all seem to find this trivia so thrilling, why don't we all say where we're going and what we want to achieve?' I was convinced I knew the answer to this, although I couldn't have expressed it in words.

Dave, the normally mild second violinist, piped up. 'Well, for example, we seem to spend all our time playing contemporary music even though none of us are particularly interested in it,' he said. 'It's all very fine being busy but I know that's not what I joined the quartet to do.'

This was true, as we enjoyed an unrivalled reputation in the performance of the 'difficult', and 'dissonant' contemporary string quartets that were particularly in favour with funders such as the Arts Council and the BBC at that time.

Crikey, I thought, this is getting very near the knuckle. Instantly, everyone was busily agreeing that this was absolutely *not* what being in a quartet was meant to be about.

The second violin piped up again. 'I joined the quartet to play Beethoven – not that we ever do, because we're all too frightened of it.'

This really was true. At the time, we played only one Beethoven quartet and had tacitly avoided facing up to any of the others because they were so desperately difficult – not just technically, but emotionally, with their issues of control and ensemble and so on. Within a few moments there was complete unanimity that we should be playing more Beethoven.

Perhaps unconsciously recognising that this brief taste of liberty was allowing the others to articulate their frustrations about me, and feeling threatened, I instinctively reclaimed my decisive leadership role.

The popular voice had spoken and so I now proceeded to take the credit for initiating it, a classic democratic case of 'Wait for me – I'm your leader!'

'OK, OK,' I announced. 'If we all want to play Beethoven that's exactly what we'll do. I'm certainly not interested in being in the quartet unless we succeed in doing what's really important to us. So we'll learn all seventeen of the Beethovens and play nothing else until it's done.' This final shot was very typically 'me'. When challenged, raise the stakes.

At this point a really interesting episode of quartet behaviour began to play out. Each one of us responded instinctively according to our fundamental personality type. I find the ancient description of human beings according to four types, or temperaments, a kind of psychological shorthand, still provides a lot of practical insight. It came down to the medieval alchemists from Hippocrates and the Greeks, but has its origins in Ancient Egypt and Mesopotamia.

The viola player, Ivo, a classic melancholic type, cautious, organised and methodical, anxiously pointed out, 'Learning all this music will take a huge amount of time and that's going to cost money.' With that he promptly went off into a corner and started scribbling figures onto the back of an envelope.

As the decisive choleric type, the self-styled alpha male, I commandeered the initiative: 'If you tell me what's needed I'll sort it out – but then we'll do *all* the quartets and no quibbles.' In other words, 'I can give you what you want, but only if you follow *my* rules.'

The second violinist spoke up again. He was a fine man and a perfect second fiddle, solid, reliable, decent and mature, and sufficiently aware of his technical limitations to find fulfilment as the support act. His words carried a disturbing self-doubt that was to prove prescient. He seemed strangely fearful. 'But we'll never do it,' he kept saying. 'It's beyond us. It's more than we can achieve . . .'

Part of the challenge in finding an ideal second fiddle is that they don't all spring from the ranks of a single temperamental type. We discovered the importance of this when we later replaced our original second fiddle with a thoroughly sanguine individual who was an exasperating mixture of brilliance, unreliability and moodiness as well as being a compulsive partygoer. In this case I think our original colleague was sufficiently insecure to feel the need of a dominant leader.

My reaction was instant choleric anger. I fiercely despised any display of weakness – my mother's influence, perhaps? As usual, when it spoke, this voice was profane. 'Of course we'll fucking do it,' I told him. 'Don't be so stupid, we'll set ourselves to do it and we'll go on working till we have.'

Then, bless him, Lew, our phlegmatic, peace-loving and unassertive cellist, piped up. 'Well, as long as everyone else really wants to do them, then of course I'd love to.' He gave a momentary glance of concern towards his lifelong friend the second fiddle, and also to me whom he wanted so much to live up to.

This was probably the only really honest conversation we ever had in the quartet. Everything else was negotiated around the texture of our musical life and rehearsal together. Perhaps there were advantages to this, but in hindsight it is difficult not to see that we missed countless opportunities for constructive negotiation and reconciliation along the way. I must concede that the main obstacle was probably me, not by intention but by blind force of personality, which itself was more an expression of hidden weakness than of real strength.

We auction ourselves at the Queen Elizabeth Hall

Characteristically, I had made this commitment without having the slightest idea of how to fulfil it. I expected the universe to provide for me as it always did. Chatting all this over with an older friend, Michael Willis-Fleming, he became rather enthusiastic.

Michael was a lifelong member of the Study Society and a most cultured and cultivated man. I have discovered only recently that he was the scion of one of England's oldest families who came over with William the Conqueror. Eton-educated and very well-to-do – at least by my standards – he also had a great love of music.

Such was his upper-class accent and challengingly elliptical discourse, full of obscure references, that I found much of what he said quite incomprehensible. Despite all of this we used to have the most delightful conversations – leaving me with only the vaguest idea of what he had been talking about.

This was midway through the 1980s, when Margaret Thatcher was in her ascendancy, and Michael explained to me that the City was awash with money. I had no idea then what exactly the 'City' did.

'Yes,' he continued. 'The market has so much money, they don't know what to do with it. Why don't you just auction yourselves?'

'But auction what exactly?' I asked, completely confused. 'Oh, don't worry about that, there's so much money about they'll buy anything. I'll ask my friend Robert Armstrong, the Cabinet Secretary, to bid; he loves music.'

Although I never did quite comprehend what we were selling, I didn't need to be asked twice.

At a concert in the Queen Elizabeth Hall a few weeks later, I got the promoter's permission to hold an auction in the foyer immediately after the performance. A near neighbour of ours was a senior auctioneer for Sotheby's and he kindly agreed to run the bidding.

That very week the ruling Conservative party announced that in order to reduce state support and encourage corporate and private funding for the arts, the government would match-fund new sponsorship money coming into the arts through a quango called ABSA (the Association for Business Sponsorship of the Arts).

Without knowing anything more than this, I blithely announced on the radio that the government had kindly agreed to match any money we raised at the auction. I also wrote to the minister thanking him for his support. A supportive telegram arrived from him on the evening of the concert and naturally I read it out to the assembled press.

After only a few minutes the bidding reached £45,000, which was exactly the amount we had calculated was needed to subsidise our study of the Beethoven quartets. I duly stopped the sale and a lot of disappointed 'investors' went away feeling altogether perplexed.

Fortunately ABSA sent its contribution by return of post and this unusual event also attracted unprecedented levels of publicity, together with the offer of an open recording contract for Nimbus Records.

Nimbus was the most exciting label around and the only one to own its CD technology. As Michael always insisted, 'If the project is right, finding the money is always easy.' Although I lack his understanding of the mechanics, I accept the truth of this. I assume it is possible to act only once with such utter naivety. The second time around our psychology would already be spoiled by expectation and second-guessing. I suspect this is very similar to falling in love or even to the 'second simplicity'.

All that mattered to me was that we could now immerse ourselves in the repertoire we all knew was to be our most important work.

Insights from Beethoven: String Quartet in B flat, Op. 130

There is no doubt in my mind that the three years we spent learning the Beethoven quartets, together with the two more we dedicated to recording them, were the quartet's *raison d'être* and certainly the time of my own most significant development.

These seventeen quartets represent a complete summation of Beethoven's spiritual journey, starting with the set of six quartets, Op. 18, painstakingly composed in his late twenties and designed to show the world at large and Haydn in particular that a brilliant innovator and major new musical force had been unleashed on the musical world.

Poor 'Papa' Haydn, that great master maker and 'inventor' of the string quartet as a form, received the very first complete score from Beethoven, who had proved to be an ungracious pupil, having left owing Haydn tuition money.

Once he had read all six quartets through, Haydn put his pen down halfway through what was to be his final, unfinished string quartet, his Op. 103, having written underneath the final notes, 'I am finished.'

Across his leonine middle period Beethoven composed a kind of musical commentary of all that was most radical and thrilling in his soul. These are the truly amazing quartets: the three 'Rasumovsky' quartets. Op. 59, so noble and inventive that Beethoven would be considered the greatest master of this medium even had he never written any others. And to finish these middle-period quartets there is 'The Harp', Op. 74, and Op. 95, a vehement distillation of terse musical power.

The master came to compose the greatest quartets of the entire repertoire, the 'late quartets', in 1825 and 1826 when he was in miserable health: Op. 127, Op. 130, Op. 131, Op. 132 with its immense slow movement inscribed 'a prayer of thanksgiving on the recovery from illness, in the Lydian mode'; the *Grosse Fuge*, Op. 133, and finally the mysterious Op. 135, which feels like staring into a bottomless pool of water and manages to be both facile and profound all at once. Beethoven died shortly afterwards, in 1827, aged fifty-six.

These great and noble works acted as a crucible and a testing ground in which we were at last forced, kicking and screaming, to grow up.

By mentioning here just a few of the key learning moments I hope to show how interconnected were the technical, musical and emotional issues. Two incidents presented themselves with particular clarity during our struggles to learn the majestic Op. 130.

This quartet has six movements that revolve around each other like planets orbiting a sun, perfectly represented by my first coma vision, where I found myself one of a group of worshipping acolytes floating in space around a wondrous deity.

Part of the glory of the work is that Beethoven famously created two alternative finales. One is a deeply deceptive rondo, which bubbles with an irresistible enthusiasm yet dances above some unspeakable darkness. The other is the infamous *Grosse Fuge*, which is a polyphonic tour de force of vehement and frustrated anger. Beethoven was not naturally gifted in counterpoint and forced himself to study it *ad nauseam*. Despite, or perhaps because of, his limitations he eventually composed some of the most wonderful fugues ever written. This 'Great Fugue' stands like a monolith above and beyond nearly all other music with a modernity that places it far outside its own period. The choice of finale changes the centre of gravity of the whole work.

Of the middle movements the third inhabits an ambivalent musical world that is Beethoven's alone. It is simultaneously fast and slow, lyrical and contrapuntal. To make matters worse for the performers it is situated in the almost impossible key of D flat major.

String instruments play most easily and naturally in keys that include some or all of the notes of their open strings. Partly because of complexities of the Pythagorean gap, the further into the territory of multiple flats or sharps they go, the less comfortable their tonal colours sound. All the great composers understand this and deliberately choose contrasting keys to conjure up distinct emotional responses.

When Beethoven decides that a central movement of this masterpiece must be played in the most alien of keys, he immediately places the music far above and beyond the ordinary. In so doing he also renders it well-nigh unplayable because the complexities of the Pythagorean gap are multiplied between the four contrasting voices.

The awkwardness is reinforced by his multiple tempo markings – *andantino* – *quasi allegretto, ma non troppo, un poco scherzoso*, and then (in the first violin part alone) *dolce*. The instruction *andantino* is perhaps one of the most ambiguous in Western music. *Andante* translates as 'at a walking speed', but to the best of my knowledge no one has ever established whether the term *andantino* (a little *andante*) means something slightly faster or slightly slower than an *andante*.

To ensure total confusion, Beethoven carefully qualifies this uncertainty by adding the refinement *quasi allegretto* (like an *allegretto*). *Allegro* indicates brisk or lively, but no one knows whether an *allegretto* (a little *allegro*) is more or less brisk. But the master is not yet finished. He continues with *ma non troppo* (but not too much) and *un poco scherzoso* (in a slightly joking style). Finally and only for the first violin, he adds *dolce* (sweetly).

Felix Mendelssohn brilliantly observed that the 'affects' (the nature of the feelings) of music are 'too precise to express in words', but surely this is going too far.

All of this does make a kind of sense when one discovers that the music consists of multiple contrapuntal (many-voiced) strands of music weaving in and out of each other, so that each voice continually swaps roles with the others.

The problems present themselves immediately. The first violin, the leader, begins the movement with a single legato note. The second violin and viola then enter together in a form of stately dance rhythm, while the cellist very soon sets out on a dance of his own.

The passivity of this first musical utterance, devoid of rhythm or contour, renders the leader impotent to control or shape subsequent events – I know this because for many futile weeks in rehearsal I tried really hard to do just that.

Over and over again I attempted subtly to indicate the tempo. By now, fifteen or so years into our career (Sidney Griller would have approved), this was not some crude semaphore but a breath that would empathically convey both the speed and the emotional mood of the music.

Over and over again I attempted to distil my vision of the piece into this single note and over and over again I failed to inspire my colleagues into any vestige of ensemble. In desperation I then tried to *think* the quaver movement of the second violin and viola. But this again proved impossibly elusive because consciously thinking the wrong rhythmic subdivision made my own line agitated and impure.

When everyone's exasperation had reached boiling point the second fiddle and the violist rose in rebellion, arguing that since they had the first moving part it must be their role to initiate the tempo. I conceded, grudgingly, and we set off again into another futile round of rehearsal. Every once in a while they succeeded in setting a joint tempo (in quavers, as their parts demanded) but the musical style was disastrous. At long last, after we had become completely disenchanted with this approach, even our sweet-natured phlegmatic cellist was moved to speak up.

With an uncharacteristic assertiveness born of long suffering, he seized the initiative and pointed out that since he had the fastest notes, control of the tempo inevitably fell to him, irrespective of any superfluous theorising on our part.

We now began the laborious task of reconfiguring our musical and personal interactions to allow for the cellist's leadership. He tripped along confidently enough in semi-quavers but though the outcome was certainly different, it was still unsatisfactory – albeit in a different way.

At our wits' end, I summed up our situation. 'It seems to me', I said, 'that we have honestly attempted to resolve and prepare this movement as well as we possibly can – but I think we have to accept that if we can't play this movement we're just not destined to perform the Beethoven cycle – and we should accept that.'

Dispiritedly, everyone agreed. The facts were incontrovertible. Then, out of nowhere, the second violinist spoke. This was not someone inclined to flights of fancy; in fact he was rather a stolid personality.

'I want to make a suggestion,' he said. 'I propose that we play it just once more without saying anything. If it doesn't work we'll simply give up the idea of playing the Beethovens and never say another word about it.'

We all groaned.

'What's the point of doing it again?' I moaned.

But he was adamant. Nobody had a better idea, and so with resignation and without further discussion, we buckled down to yet another play-through.

Within a few bars it became absolutely obvious that this was something entirely new. Like magic, the different musical lines integrated and somehow complemented each other – even the vexed intonation was reconciled. As we played I remember studiously avoiding eye contact; God forbid that a careless self-congratulatory glance should break the magic spell.

Just beyond halfway through I can recall beginning to tense up, anxious that I might inadvertently spoil this eggshell perfection. But even harbouring this fear we all successfully negotiated the whole movement.

The last notes of the movement make an ironic final musical gesture as if the composer is sharing some divine joke. This punctuates the end of the music like a delicious full stop. On this occasion even this curious gesture unfolded with a thoroughly delightful sense of light-hearted grace. As we finished, we all drew a joyful breath of satisfaction and pleasure, and then we all turned in our seats and as one voice said to each other, 'There you are – I was right!'

Cavatina

One of the most beautiful rewards and moments of solace that arose for us as a quartet occurred one afternoon when, exhausted and frustrated, we were rehearsing the *Cavatina*, the fifth movement of Beethoven's String Quartet in B flat major, Op. 130.

The *Cavatina* is for many the emotional kernel of Beethoven's late quartets and the most beautiful expression of the spiritual stated with the utmost brevity – like some exquisite sonnet or haiku. In complete contrast to the preceding movements, its challenge lies in its deceptive simplicity. The same simplicity as prayer, yet its many tenuous strands interweave so that only a complete unanimity of emotional state between the players can reveal its immensity.

At its mid-point there is a sudden brief and emotionally shattering episode in which all sense of harmonic and melodic coherence is suddenly ripped away. This passage stands above all music and beyond time. The only direction is *Beklemmt* ('sorrowful or distraught of heart'). A single precious fragment that tells us that the composer knew only too well the utter abandonment of lost love.

Beethoven's friend, Ignaz Schuppanzigh, the leader of the quartet who attempted the first performance of Op. 130, describes watching the deaf composer sitting alone, reading the score of the *Cavatina*, weeping as he read. Beethoven is said to have considered it to be his single greatest musical achievement.

For some unaccountable reason, at the end of one long afternoon of stressful rehearsal, we decided to attempt this movement just once more. From the first note it was clear that we had collectively entered an entirely different emotional state. We played as if in joint contemplation and when at last the music faded away, without a word, we each simply got up and left.

The intensity and honesty of relationship we needed was found only as we were preparing to depart. As with so many things in life, 'the candle burns brightest just before it goes out'. It was only as we reached the end of such a difficult day that we were able to 'let go' of the emotional issues that had been holding us back.

This is the special piquancy that accrues within activities that we are leaving for ever – a quality I can certainly now attest to when facing the end of all things.

A few years later, our second violinist, who had been a founder member and staunch companion for some twenty years, left the quartet in difficult circumstances. Although my sense of loss was intense I found myself incapable of feeling anything but love for him afterwards because of this single shared transcendent experience.

Once we experience the absolute, all else becomes reframed and strangely shadowy. Dying also has that effect most power-fully. This shared apotheosis, uniquely present throughout a whole musical movement, left innumerable shards of con-solation as it passed.

When I asked my old mentor Clifford Curzon what he considered to be the ultimate reward of music he replied, 'Consolation.'

Terribly young and naive at the time I was clumsy enough to ask, 'A consolation for what?'

With a look of infinite resignation he replied quietly, 'For life, Paul, for life.'

What is an ensemble?

I longed to know from within other people's experience the kind of unconditional love that most of us experience *in utero* and at our mother's breast. Of course I also aspired to achieve this in the intimacies of physical love but actually came closest within music.

We should not be surprised that many of the chemical markers of intimacy, pleasure and trust such as oxytocin, the opioids and serotonin are implicated in the musical reward system in the brain. That music can mimic, reflect and stimulate loving behaviour is a given – 'the food of love' indeed.

Musical language and discourse are almost embarrassingly abundant with erotic overtones and references. The most staid professional orchestra, bored in a rehearsal and covertly watching the clock, will not even twitch when instructed by the conductor to 'make the climax more intense in bar twenty-six', or to 'come together at the beginning of the mounting phrases in the exposition'.

Although it continues to embarrass some colleagues I remain convinced that the language of music is *essentially erotic*. Like sex, it is designed by nature to be intimately stimulating and gesturally based in its performance. Music is probably one of the most arousing behaviours that 'civilised' human beings can publicly engage in and shares the characteristic of dance so wittily captured by the remark attributed to George Bernard Shaw that 'dancing is a vertical expression of a horizontal desire'.

So it must be a matter of wonder when a small group of people elect to lock themselves away for many hours a day refining these intensely intimate and highly ritualised behaviours. Freud would undoubtedly contest that it is exactly in this ritualisation that the civilising sublimation of the original impulse takes place, and unless we can embrace the notion of a spiritual impulse, which Freud denied (until shortly before he died), we still have no better explanation.

However, I should say that while the quartet might have been using and developing so-called 'feminine' sensibilities, there was never a single moment when the relationship between us felt remotely sexualised. Erotic certainly, but not sexual.

The individual and the group

Naturally gifted players have certain intrinsic mannerisms that make their playing distinctive and interesting. Yet in order to give a full contribution to an ensemble it is necessary to sacrifice some of this individuality for the greater good of the ensemble.

Not surprisingly, only a very special type of person and player is able and willing to do this. Beethoven's quartets demand this sacrifice at the very deepest level; each player makes a 'gift' of him- or herself to his or her colleagues. In this sense, playing Beethoven becomes possible only when everybody is in a willing state of maximum discomfort. Without such tension there is no music – and certainly none of Beethoven's music, as he begins where others leave off.

Along the way, peer pressure and the music itself combine together to oblige each personality and player to demonstrate and master his or her least comfortable mode. The diffident find themselves obliged to dominate and lead and, conversely, the naturally dominant must learn to yield and support the others. The bold become meek and the forthright assume discretion. The loud, the quiet and the clumsy are all finessed. I have an intimation that playing the major Shakespeare roles could have a similar transforming effect on those actors who are able to rise to them.

I must acknowledge that, after we had finished learning the Beethoven quartets and had recorded and performed the complete cycle together many times, we found it difficult to scale down to other, less demanding composers.

Music that did not challenge us by stretching and stressing us beyond our limits tended to feel insubstantial, and it was several years before I realised that living at such an intense pitch is addictive and not quite normal.

The battle for the imagination

As it develops its own style, a quartet is engaged in a continual tidal struggle, which I consider to be a battle for the imagination.

All significant musical works evoke their own emotional and spiritual world. The finest music describes subtle emotional states with such precision that without them we might not know that such conditions can even exist. Music can also simultaneously evoke extraordinarily complex combinations of positive and negative emotions. This is how – and to an extent also why – we can enjoy listening to melancholy music.

When we were working with the fabulously gifted Indian classical musician Wajahat Khan, he told us that in his tradition, 'happy' and 'sad' were not accepted categories, whereas 'deep' was. The novelty of this view to a Western sensibility is a reminder that our culture puts enormous and indiscriminate store by the entire gamut of passing emotions and that we tend to be wholly convinced of the 'reality' of each one for as long as we remain in its grip. The notion that emotions, like ideas, can, and perhaps should, be regarded according to a scale of value and meaning is no longer much recognised. Music surely teaches us the ephemeral quality of emotions, not by considering them all to be facile or insincere but by reminding us of their fleeting nature.

There is also immense comfort to be discovered in the realisation that such extraordinary beauty and joy can spring from melancholy.

Interpretation: String Quartet in C sharp minor,
   Op. 131
First movement: Adagio, ma non troppo e molto
   espressivo

The opening slow fugue of Op. 131 is as poignant as music can be, but in turning such sadness into the building blocks of a formal fugue, Beethoven places desolation into a quite different context. It is as if the pain of loss or sadness produces the stones of a cathedral as well as the energy and drive to build it – which was of course the case for true Christian believers.

Poor Beethoven knew only too well the miseries of lost love (the 'immortal beloved') and suffered an unhappy childhood with an abusive father. As he longed for an emotional intimacy that was probably never possible, his life was made all the more difficult by his early deafness and a fiercely demanding nature. All this can be intuited from playing his music.

Beethoven was a 'believer' but of a more modern kind than most of his contemporaries. For him, the Godhead had also to be found within, and the epic journey from the initial knotted misery of Op. 131 to the final rapturous vehemence of its finale is one of release from depression into a personal liberty and freedom of the spirit – very much at variance with Bach's more orthodox faith.

Op. 131 begins with the first violin playing the fugue subject, which is derived from the same four-note harmonic minor tetrachord on which virtually all the late quartets are based.

In this case it is the leader who sets the tone for the whole work. These few notes gain even greater significance when one realises that the whole piece has to be played without a break, each successive movement springing directly from the one before. To capture this opening mood, tempo and style are therefore absolutely critical. To make matters even more challenging, this movement is in C sharp minor, a key so alien as to hardly exist anywhere else in the whole string quartet repertoire.

Long before going onstage the first violin must be inhabiting this opening phrase and internally imaging the peculiar and distinctive sound world of its exotic key. This very first phrase immediately demands a rapid crescendo and sforzando. Typical of this extraordinary, contradictory man, Beethoven offers no opening dynamic marking, but the extended, unwinding counterpoint that follows this strangely distorted beginning is overwhelmingly marked *piano*, which suggests that the first note should also begin quietly before its precipitous dynamic rise.

Another typical ambiguity is that Beethoven marks the score as being in split common time. That is, in two minims to the bar rather than the much more common four crotchet beats. This implicit minim pulse places the counterpoint firmly in an earlier, archaic musical world – and Beethoven acknowledged that before embarking on these compositions, he had made an exhaustive study of Palestrina's contrapuntal style and technique. All of these issues warrant demanding discussion and exploration in rehearsal.

Actually, just playing the movement in tune is a significant issue in itself. The key of C sharp minor takes no hostages, forcing the open strings of all the instruments into very odd relationships with its tonic note. In a sense this movement – full of airy gravitas – defies grounding.

After much struggle we concluded that the only way to capture the exact tempo and feeling of this movement was to *think* in crotchets while *playing* the extended themes in minims. This produced a spacious, uncluttered ambience rather along the lines of Palestrina's broad counterpoint.

Negotiation and rehearsal

Without a most painstakingly pre-negotiated agreement of rhythmic intent this movement is unplayable. Unless everyone is fully alert and functioning along exactly parallel lines of thought the performance simply cannot be sustained.

Another feature that distinguishes this opening fugue is the constant, exaggerated punctuation of accents coupled with the abrupt drops in dynamic level of the *subito piano*s. Although with sufficient familiarity these become more comfortable, they are actually very odd and, given the apparent shapes of the phrases, how to play them is far from obvious.

Beethoven was dismissively rude about having to provide such precise expression and dynamic markings, insisting scornfully that he was obliged to do so 'only because of the wilful stupidity of players who seemed incapable of responding to the clear musical implications of the musical phrases'.

Even these days there is nothing self-evident about his phrase lengths, so it is no wonder that his terrified contemporaries floundered so wretchedly. After two years of studying this work, his devoted friend Schuppanzigh said, 'While it has passages of great beauty, much of it remains utterly incomprehensible!'

In the case of Op. 131 it is the leader's task to set in train everything that unfolds over the following thirty-five minutes of unparalleled, profound and beautiful music. For the first violin, every nuance is literally as well as metaphorically 'in your hands'. Even within the rarefied world of the string quartet repertoire there exists only a handful of masterpieces in which such moral, noumenal moments as that telling first phrase abound. Such works are perhaps created only by people who are fully conscious of what they are doing and are designed to have a life-changing impact when their interpretation in performance matches their composition.

Establishing tempo

I calculated that it had taken us 180 hours of joint rehearsal to prepare Op. 74, 'The Harp', for our first performance.

I think this was multiplied by a factor of ten when we came to learn the late quartets. They are just as technically demanding as Beethoven's earlier quartets but yet more complex and difficult to comprehend. Every nuance had to be thrashed out, discussed, debated, discarded and reshaped hundreds of times before a consensus could be achieved – and only then did the tempo integration and relationships begin to reveal themselves. I found this to be a particularly rewarding period in our preparation. Only after some weeks into each work would we reach a threshold where the emotions, technique and musical demands of the piece would come together so that we could all recognise the underlying tempo relationships that held the musical fabric together.

The layman might presume that this process could be simplified merely by studying the established speeds of previous great performances, but it simply doesn't work that way – and it shouldn't, because until a group has developed its own unique weight, style and approach there *is* no tempo. There may be speeds – but the speed of a metronome has virtually nothing to do with the tempo of an interpretation. The 'speed' of a performance relates to its calibrated pulse, just as one might measure the duration of a race. But the performance tempo of an interpretation refers to something more akin to its heartbeat, flow, breathing and gait. We resorted to the metronome throughout our rehearsals but, according to our level of musical understanding at the time, this could prove to be useful, or just mindless and irritating. Only when every variable had been explored and negotiated could we try to capture our tempos as metronomic measurements of speed.

Nevertheless, simply reproducing the speeds that had previously worked wonderfully did not guarantee a perfect performance, because all the other circumstances were never identical – our feelings, the humidity of the room and weight of the instrument, the acoustic and so on. Anyway, what is the value of strict repetition in performance? The whole purpose of music-making is to allow the spirit of spontaneous invention to keep the music alive.

Tempo relationships

One afternoon, several years into our intensive Beethoven studies, when we were in the midst of Op. 131, Ivo, our 'melancholic' violist, suddenly insisted that we must calculate and codify the exact tempo relationships of the piece. He was clearly on the brink of some kind of mathematical and musical breakthrough and was already scribbling numbers down on a piece of paper.

'Listen,' he said, 'it all works perfectly if you take the quaver beats as the base unit and calculate everything from that, bearing in mind that the second movement stands in a ratio of 3:2 to the first. So, crotchet = 78 makes each quaver 156. This means that at the same tempo, a dotted crotchet beat in the complex 3 tempo (6/8) of the second movement = 52. Dividing this by two = 26 and take it away from the 156 = 130.'

I still have no idea how well these ratios stand up to scrutiny, but the alignments are compelling, as was the feeling we shared that there must be some inner rhythmical coherence to the way the music best unfolded.

For non-musicians I should define the term *hemiola*, which underlies the rhythmic impulse of much Western music. A hemiola exploits the fact that some patterns of notes can be grouped differently so as to create a different metre or pulse.

For example, when a piece is marked 6/8, each bar will contain six equal quaver notes. But these six notes can be played as either two sets of three or as three sets of two: 3 x 2 gives three crotchets in a bar (two quavers in each crotchet) whereas 2 x 3 gives two dotted crotchets in a bar (three quavers in each dotted crotchet). Imagine three couples dancing together, six dancers in all. They can dance either as three couples or join hands into two groups of three people.

Composers and performers often present these options in such a way as to create ambiguous rhythms. Once again, notes behave just like groups of people or families and their ever-changing liaisons are infinitely fascinating.

Many baroque dance forms such as the gigue rely on a constant interplay of these two equally valid readings of a 6/8 rhythm and alternating between them lends the music a lilting and often humorous playfulness.

It is interesting to note that the same mathematical relationships also define the intervals of the musical scale – as in the ratios between the frequencies (vibrations) of the notes: 1:2 = the octave interval and 2:3 = the 'perfect' fifth.[*]

In this way the internal rhythms of music and all its actual pitches and harmonies are inherently mathematically related. Throughout the ages mystics have often pointed out this congruence to demonstrate that music is a perfect reflection of the laws that underpin the whole universe – and, from this, that everything in the universe is vibrational.

---

[*] Frequency is of course just 'rhythm' at a higher level. The frequency of musical notes is so fast that the ear perceives it as a tone, in cycles per second, rather than a pulse, in beats per minute.

Second movement: Allegro molto vivace

Following the anguished fugal opening movement, the second movement begins in a far more optimistic mood – and significantly it is in D major. Although D is immediately adjacent to C sharp, the two keys can barely cohabit. Open, cheerful D major has an utterly different mood, association and colour from the strange and alienated C sharp minor. All the instruments have a D string, so they all resonate together sympathetically and warmly in the key of D.

To add to this sense of a lifting of the spirits this movement is just that – *moving* – flowing and tripping along in 6/8, often almost dancing.

The other feature that gives this music so much energy is its ever-shifting tonality. In this case, each modulation and most of the passage-work creates an illusion of forever 'lifting off' in a rising emotional exuberance. In direct contrast to the suppressed anguish of the first movement, the dynamics are curiously playful and yet rather lumpen at the same time – just like the composer himself when in a jolly mood or slightly drunk, a condition that by all accounts was by no means unusual. Beethoven's music is often filled with this rather knockabout good humour, although it is never allowed to become merely trite.

Some passages in this movement have an almost comical obsession, unnaturally stressing the middle of the bar rather than the beginning. This is so exaggerated that at one point in the final third of the movement Beethoven apparently allows himself to get 'stuck', trying desperately to insist that the second beat is actually the first, and the effect suggests an angry bear trying to shake off a swarm of attacking bees.

One of the qualities of music is that if it keeps on insisting on it, the listener can quite quickly be made to hear the wrong note as 'home' – rather like an over-assertive individual constantly banging on the table while maintaining that black is white, so that the listener is finally browbeaten into submission.

With Beethoven having now broken both the sense of tonality and the rhythmic pulse, the audience is left entirely at sea, all expectations and assumptions thwarted. Without realising it (as with all his late-period masterpieces), we are being carefully and precisely set up and inwardly prepared for a complete psychological shift – an inner migration to an entirely new world.

This was also the intention of Gurdjieff's mysterious symbolic writing and a similar method of inner transformation was taught in practice by Dr Roles's school. The purpose of such psychological techniques is gradually to oblige the individual to question all his inner assumptions and to seek to rebuild himself from an objective basis. In an esoteric school it is considered essential to undertake this work together with one's fellows under the guidance of a trusted teacher before each student can eventually bring his efforts to serve the 'world' – which is partially what this book is about. Another aspect of this 'service' was fulfilled during my many years as an early exponent of the effects and relations of music to brain function.

The musical world has very similar structures to traditional esoteric schooling and at one time, not even that long ago, they were almost certainly conjoined. My beloved colleagues were the quartet; Clifford Curzon and a few others were my teachers, while our career as performers hopefully made some contribution to the larger community. This personal archetypal journey is mirrored in the music itself. Moving from the personal into relationship via the mystery of symbolic language offers a magical transformation that transports us directly into a far more beautiful and moral world. I see this as exactly the journey we must all make, not only throughout life but at the moment of death. In the musical domain, Beethoven was the master potter taking whatever clay he had to work with and transforming it into vessels of purpose, value and beauty.

Having now destroyed the defensive carapace of our psychology, from here on the music produces one bizarre and beautiful vision after another, from the comical to the ironic, the ambivalent and the resolute.

Perhaps the greatest wonder is that despite its vast array and variety the music is so subtly integrated into a whole that at some incalculable level each and every note is miraculously connected and self-reflective. As with life, it is the music itself that provides the key to its own mysteries.

Because of this, the late quartets finally reveal their remarkable interconnectedness and full depth of meaning only when each is understood in the context of the others.

Tempo relationships in Op. 131

Ivo's realisation of the underlying tempo relationships of the varied musical episodes and movements of Op. 131 holds good for many other composers. Bach and Brahms spring immediately to mind, although in Bach's case it is hard to tell to what extent he was *consciously* applying this principle. So much of his music is based on dance forms that inherently reflect the natural repertoire of body rhythms.

For many years, and not only in playing Beethoven, we were rigorous about applying these mathematical pulse relationships to our performances. This certainly made them highly integrated, although possibly this was at the cost of losing some emotional flexibility.

If we are to accept that Beethoven was probably bipolar, much of the emotion of his musical journey was, to some extent at least, driven by the instability of his condition. While the intellect is drawn to clear relationships, the autonomic (emotional– instinctive) nervous system is far more nuanced and ambiguous.

Nevertheless, there can be no doubt that the music traces an almost graphic expansion from darkest depression to ecstatic joy and I am convinced that his aim was to construct music of such objectivity that it would convey both extremes.

This is perhaps why there is so much legitimate variation between different musical interpretations – a player can be principally inspired by either the mind or the heart and only the very best bring head, heart and hand together in what can now be described as an unusual but transcendent unity of the two hemispheres of the brain.

Where is home?

The magnificent finale of Op. 131 travels with inevitability from urgent aspiration to a final frantic joy. The idea of the key of C sharp minor representing a place of certainty is almost unimaginable. But Beethoven is utterly adamant and in this movement C sharp is virtually banged into us – like a nail being hammered into a log – and in the face of such certainty it is impossible to resist. The great man is now going to prove that black is white and before we know it we are swept up in this 'contrary' world view.

Having driven the nail of C sharp deep into our very souls he now begins to rail against it. Time and again the music tries to escape, fleeing through one key after another, sometimes, like a hunted animal, hiding momentarily in some other sheltering key but to no avail. There is no refuge. The music may flow, it may plead, it may search and endlessly explore but all is futile. C sharp is now our 'home'. The more the music seems to protest, the greater our certainty.

Even reintroducing the desperately broken fragments of the opening fugal subject serves only to hurl yet more material into the final maelstrom. C sharp is now the centre of the universe and everything must finally be drawn there. After a final and almost pathetically broken reprise, the whole emotional edifice tenuously but irresistibly finishes with three brusque chords in C sharp major!

So is *that* what all this was about? Dear, good, unhappy man – for just three notes the tortured Beethoven smiles on us and, we hope, on himself.

We know that Beethoven devoted enormous effort to comprehending the inner secrets of perfect counterpoint, as did many others who came after him, but no other composer has ever approached his amazing achievement in marrying the cool objectivity of the Renaissance masters to the deeply passionate world of the subjective imagination.

This is why we recognise in Beethoven the true spirit of Romanticism.

When, oh when shall I experience *that overwhelming joy once more in the temples of man or of nature? Never? Oh God, that would be too hard. Let me have, I pray thee, just one more day of pure Joy.*

Beethoven, *Heiligenstadt Testament*

The role of interpretation

I hope this brief summary of some of the elements involved in making an interpretation may offer a glimpse into the process of learning a complex score. This section is the only one not to reference any of my coma visions, for unlike the numerous incomprehensible events in my life that do demand interpretation, working within the quartet was *itself* the act of interpretation.

Things already understood need no additional mystery but act naturally as guides towards clarification of the ineffable.

This poem by A. J. Pinching asks about the preconceptual moment when the composer is imagined by the performer:

& ante

What just denoted walking pace,
the leisured middle movement stroll, becomes –
with an exquisite error of transcription – the question:
'And before?' Nothing so simple as: 'And then?'

To find a way into this mystery,
we could walk awhile, and then look back,
triangulate future and present
towards a not yet remembered past.

The sonata encompasses familiar patterns,
flowing and developing in its path –
but is this really 'And before?',
or just the prelude to a question?

& ante askes about the preconceptual moment
when the composer is imagined by the performer.

Group breakdown

As we were completing the recordings of our Beethoven quartet cycle an authoritative inner voice directed me, 'Now you have finished the Beethovens, you have no excuse to find anything frightening ever again.'

I thought about this a great deal and concluded that the thing I most feared was the possibility of losing the quartet. It dawned on me that here was the opportunity to change the pattern of our relationship. After all, it was what we had just spent well over five years doing while working on the Beethovens.

I announced to my colleagues that, since we had now successfully negotiated the repertoire that represented the pinnacle of our life's ambition, I no longer felt obliged to act as their big brother or father figure and would not be doing so any more. The results were shocking.

I had assumed that we had all been on the same journey, but seemingly this was not the case at all – or was our journey shared but not its destination? To me, it was clear that the process of growing up we had been engaged on meant that from this point I could cease to direct them and they would all now wish to take responsibility for their own lives and incomes.

It soon became obvious that my colleagues harboured no such aspirations. The violist and cellist insisted that they were broke after the Beethoven years and could afford to continue only if they sold their London homes and went to live in the countryside.

After a while my three colleagues were in agreement and so, most unwillingly, I too agreed to move house. Inwardly I was convinced that this financial angst was only a metaphor for more fundamental, emotional problems. The violist and I ended up moving near to Oxford while the second fiddle and the cellist had marital breakdowns instead.

Out of allegiance to the violist I attempted to rehearse wherever was most convenient. This involved endless drives to London, which I hated. To make matters worse, the violist and cellist now began to earn the bulk of their income by doing commercial recording sessions. I tried to join them but loathed it. Although the players were skilled, the music and general approach were solely money-oriented and I simply could not comprehend why anyone who had spent so much time in the company of Beethoven would do such a thing – and I still do not understand it.

I was convinced that now we had ascended Parnassus the whole world would lie at our feet. I was quite wrong.

The energy that had lifted us like a great wave onwards and through the Beethoven seasons seemed suddenly to seep away – as did our audiences. But I was not thinking about audiences nor indeed of anything much beyond the desire to reap the benefits of our hard-won excellence and richer musical insight.

Before long – and just as he had predicted when we first embarked on our great journey – the second fiddle player also began to melt away. His marriage collapsed and with it so did he. He began to speak of giving up the violin entirely and developed strange lumps all over his back, followed by mysteriously disabling muscular problems. He managed one last Beethoven cycle and then left – first his wife and family, and then the country.

Although we had weathered a similar loss when we were about ten years into the quartet's life, this felt like a bereavement. Despite our managing to persevere without him for a further twenty years, it was never the same as before.

He had never been the best or most scintillating player but he had been the mortar that held us all together. There were many aspects of the quartet's breakdown that were to find echoes in my later illness and I now wonder whether my need to hold on to the ensemble at this time played a part in the final breakdown of my health. There had always been plenty of stress but from this time onwards I felt locked into an endless cycle of diminishing returns.

All of this precipitated a classic mid-life crisis, which I didn't in any way see coming towards me.

Fool that I was, I was convinced that the completion of the Beethovens and the high point of playing and confidence this had created within me (and I presumed within the group) was simply the launchpad for another and higher level of achievement. I suppose in a way it was but, as they say, 'If you want to make God laugh – tell him your plans.'

My quietly perceptive spiritual mentor at the Study Society, Professor Richard Guyatt,* instantly recognising that I had

* Dickie was retired from being Rector of the Royal College of Art, where he had personally invented and gone on to establish the then

arrived at one of life's major crossroads, took me aside one day to enquire, 'Now you have got all this done I presume you can finish with the quartet and concentrate on your spiritual work.'

With the wisdom of hindsight I am sure he was right, but my mind was simply not yet ready to turn in that direction.

Now with shame I recall being completely taken aback by his question, and his obvious disappointment, because nothing was further from my mind.

Very quickly everything seemed to start falling apart.

A personal crisis

In a desperate quandary, I eventually received yet another distinct and authoritative directive in the guise of a clear internal voice. Up to this point in my life I had always relied on such spontaneous 'interventions' to direct my actions.

But the injunction it gave me now seemed entirely unacceptable, not only for myself but for others, and after an intense inner struggle I decided not to follow this supposedly 'higher' voice – a decision that immediately threw me into a violent and profoundly suicidal state.

I simply did not want to live without access to my inner guide and what had until now been an open connection with the miraculous. The noumenal had always felt much more real than ordinary life and there seemed no point in trying to live without this guiding influence. I decided to kill myself and one night made detailed plans to do so. In the course of

entirely radical concept of 'graphic design' in the post-war period. He had also been a longtime pupil of P. D. Ouspensky and Francis Roles.

this dreadful night I experienced two horrific visions. I saw two devils.

The first seems easily interpreted as he was, in a very literal sense, a horny devil. Muscular and powerful, he was a dark livid red, larger than human and covered all over in grotesque, backward-pointing, black thorns, or horns, particularly on his swollen penis – so that he would inevitably rip and tear anything he sexually possessed.

This terrifying creature was immediately followed by another diabolical figure, even more grotesque. The second devil was also bright red but smooth-skinned, soft and plump like a revoltingly swollen German sausage. To my horror he was gradually immersing himself in a bath of boiling water. As he did so, inch by inch, he was laughing horribly through his ghastly agony. Clearly the pain *was* his pleasure.

I realised that suicide could offer no escape. These two appalling aspects of myself would still be waiting and, once dead, there would no longer be any opportunity to change myself or lose them. The only grim and intolerable alternative was to try to accept my lot and learn to live an ordinary life, but I had no idea at all of how to do this. The prospect cast me into deep depression.

In desperation I turned to a therapist, who among other things recommended I read Carl Jung's autobiographical *Memories, Dreams, Reflections*. I found Jung's honesty wonderfully refreshing and made a particular note of the passage where, in a dream, he describes seeing his own doctor in his archetypal form. Jung made a great point of saying that having a vision of any person in this archetypal form always indicates their imminent death.

I dream of Manoug

The night after reading this I had a vivid dream of Manoug Parikian, who had hardly crossed my mind since our acrimonious parting so many years before.

Intensely disturbed and impressionable at this time, I insisted that my wife and I should go and visit him the following day. We were living in London at the time and I assumed that Manoug was still at his beautiful old rectory outside Oxford.

We arrived without having called ahead. I left my wife in the car and went to reintroduce myself to Manoug. He seemed very quiet and I made a point, not of apologising, but of expressing my pleasure at seeing him again, saying I would love him to come and hear the quartet play whenever he wished. He seemed rather nonplussed and mentioned that he had not been well. After parting most amicably we went home, and that night I dreamt of him again. This time, as he walked by, he was smiling warmly, not at me, but at other people I could not see, standing behind my right shoulder.

The next evening we watched a television programme featuring four famous violinists, all of whom played a Stradivarius instrument. Each soloist played one of Vivaldi's *Four Seasons*. Manoug was one of these virtuosos, and before the performance began it was announced that the recording would be aired as a memorial to Manoug, who had died that day.

I have to feel that this episode was as close to direct intervention from an external spiritual source as it is possible to get.

The beginning of the end

Eventually, nearly thirty years into the quartet's career, we had our only spectacular onstage catastrophe. It took place at the University of Lancaster, where for almost seventeen years we been the resident quartet.

The professor in charge, Denis McCaldin, was a delightful man who had often gone out of his way to help us. He had written to me well in advance to explain that as our next concert was being sponsored by a French company, an all-French programme was needed. My immediate choice of the Ravel Quartet (a stalwart of our repertoire) was precluded as we had performed it at the university only a few weeks earlier. So on this occasion Denis requested the Debussy Quartet. Having placed his letter carefully on the mantelpiece I then forgot all about it and asked my colleagues to prepare the Ravel.

On the afternoon of the concert, as we were happily rehearsing the Ravel, Denis dropped in to see us. He was naturally aghast when he realised we had brought the wrong programme and begged us to play the Debussy Quartet instead. As soon as he left the hall my colleagues all agreed, to my amazement, that in the circumstances we should certainly play the Debussy. I was horrified. I never played without thorough and painstaking rehearsal and preparation, but each of my colleagues presented compelling reasons why we should comply.

Our glamorous and feisty new second violinist, who was never much enamoured of rehearsals, announced that since she was quite happy to play the Debussy she felt I really ought to be able to do the same. 'After all,' she said, 'you've probably played it two hundred times more than me.' While this was factually true, I could not agree with her logic. We had indeed performed and broadcast the Debussy only a few weeks earlier but I felt we had played it very badly due to lack of rehearsal.

This tension between us continued for as long as we played together. Later on, when she had spent some time leading an ensemble of her own, she would come and tell me how hard leading was and how vital proper rehearsal was to produce a fine result.

Our fine viola player, an individual of great gravitas and moral compass, had a completely different, albeit equally offensive, take on the situation. 'Well, since this mistake is clearly entirely of your making and I know I can play my part perfectly well, it's quite obvious we'll have to play it.'

This revealed a whole history of ill feeling and stored-up resentment between us, which I had not been able to articulate or attempt to resolve. It seemed to me that one player believing he could play his part well enough took no account of the responsibilities of the other players to the work and to each other.

Sadly, for me, the *coup de grâce* came from our cellist, who for half a lifetime had stood by me through thick and thin. Clearly anguished, he chose, as so often, a more pragmatic perspective: 'Truthfully, I'm really hard up and I need the money. So for God's sake let's just play the bloody Debussy – after all, we know it and it'll be good enough.'

I recognised immediately that for the first time the balance of power had shifted entirely away from me. I found myself in a deep crisis, distraught and out of control. Until this moment I had always been able to impose my will, albeit with ever more elaborate strategies of convenience and political manipulation, rationalising these compromises, half-truths and power games to myself as being for the higher good – the good of the quartet itself.

By then I certainly understood that sustaining leadership meant having to choose between being loved and being followed – much as we might wish for both. The basic dilemma is as much one of 'following' as it is of 'leading' because followers avoid personal responsibility by having decisions made for them but inevitably they end up blaming the leader for whatever transpires. These relationship structures are as old as humanity and neither leaders nor their followers can escape the consequences.

This superb string quartet, in which we had begun as friends – after I slowly discovered what friends were – and had grown to become comrades and even something approaching siblings, had now evolved into something simultaneously abusive and servile. It was like a scene from *Animal Farm* and I recognised myself as having become the abusive pig, bullying a previously acquiescent bovine herd.

This was a shattering realisation. I had formed the quartet in the belief that it might come to be an ideal Platonic academy with music rather than words as its currency of debate, deceiving myself into believing that we could be a 'leaderless group' along the lines of my father's high-minded socialist aspirations. Instead, as so many esoteric teachings point out about so much of human endeavour, we were now facing in precisely the opposite direction from when we had set out.

In the event, the first half of the concert went to plan but after a greatly extended interval during which I desperately tried to process all these terrible thoughts and feelings, I found myself physically unable to lift my violin out of its case. It was as if a bomb had hit me. I could only suppose that my total inability to perform was the voice of my conscience. As time passed there seemed no other choice but to drag myself on stage to apologise and beg the understandably nonplussed audience to forgive my inability to carry on and complete the programme.

It was clear that the disillusionment and personal loss arising from this traumatic event were the manifestation of a far deeper clash of fundamental values. All our chickens had come home to roost with a vengeance. When Dave Matthews, our original second violinist left in 1991 it was, to adapt Churchill's phrase, 'the end of the beginning'. This onstage crisis was 'the beginning of the end'.

After such public existential drama we naturally lost our residency at the university. I still went on hoping that an ongoing dialogue could develop between the players but, despite my heartfelt cajoling and pleading, the others made it abundantly clear that this was just not going to happen. They seemed content simply to ignore the whole event. I felt sick and in desperation urged that we all enter group therapy but this suggestion too was resoundingly dismissed.

The onstage crisis had been perfectly archetypal in terms of group dynamics. As a visiting professor at Copenhagen Business School, working with Professor Rob Austin and Shannon O'Donnell, I developed the event into a 'business case' for the Harvard Business School. For a few very happy weeks, I presented it to their brilliant young class of prospective executive leaders. After laying out the essential elements of the crisis, the presentation finished with the classic HBS question: 'What did Robertson do next?' About a third of the students quite naturally assumed I had compromised and performed the Debussy. Others avoided speculation, and only a very few correctly predicted that I had refused to play and left the stage.

Quite what the best solution might have been I still cannot say. I could persuade myself that by honouring my own conscience I had remained in possession of the moral high ground – but in many ways it was a pyrrhic victory and left me feeling hollow. If the life and integrity of the quartet really was the 'highest good' I had always sought to maintain, it followed that my refusal to compromise my own ideals had certainly, in that sense at least, been destructive. On the other hand, it might also have been the case that the tensions between us had crystallised to such an extent that this sudden and violent resolution was inevitable and could occur only by my taking the active role. Whatever the final judgement might be, the paradox is a poignant one.

By now even our tensions had moved on. Angry and resentful that all our work should be discarded through an inability to listen, I was becoming increasingly conscious that our emotional deafness was also being reflected in our playing. What an indictment for the members of a string quartet.

At this juncture our glamorous second violinist left for family reasons and we appointed a talented young man in her place. I found 'running in' yet another new second violinist simply boring. Despite his talent, this young man seemed quite unable to take risks – perfectly understandable in a novice, but – to me – tedious. I was never a natural teacher.

Eventually, I engineered a minor onstage musical outrage. At one concert, following a particularly dismal first half, we finished the performance with Janáček's thrilling First String Quartet, 'The Kreutzer Sonata'.

This engaging and original work is based on Tolstoy's guilt-ridden erotic novella of the same name and graphically expresses Janáček's obsession with the beautiful Kamilla Stösslová, nearly forty years younger than the composer. The sexual repression of the music bursts forth in the final pages, which pulsate with passion as the smug anti-hero acts out his sexual and emotional inadequacy by murdering his wife. As this passage approached I saw the cellist and violist exchange little looks and smirk. They knew what was coming.

From here to the end the musical pulse is driven by wild ostinatos (rapid rhythmic repetitions) in the second violin part, during which the hapless second fiddle is left with a virtually unplayable attenuated passage that conveys the ghastly moral confusion of the protagonists.

I was so angry that I put my head down and charged, knowing full well that the cautious second fiddle player didn't stand a chance. But I also knew that the musical narrative demands exactly this and that even in the worst case he could not fail at least to reach the finishing line alongside us. At the end he looked spent – and livid – and hardly spoke to me for the few more months he stayed in the group.

Finally I persuaded my friend Hugh Pidgeon, a leading light in conflict resolution, to extend his existing therapeutic work with me as the sole representative of my group to a point that allowed me to persuade (and pay) my colleagues to take part in an extended performance piece he created, *The Gift*, based on a musical and verbal exposition of our conflicts.

This interesting project was supported by Lloyds Bank and we went on to perform it at various other business schools. Following its performance at Davos's 2001 World Economic Forum – where I was by then a member – the work was described as 'the most rewarding and unusual learning experience of all the forum's wonderful sessions'. Despite its many successes, my colleagues showed no interest in developing the project any further. At this point it became clear that I had to leave the group. Although I warned them of this likelihood they seemed not to hear what I was saying.

Since the outcome was now unavoidable I decided to set my own agenda. Preparing to leave took almost exactly ten years, during which time I carefully nurtured many other interests I had been neglecting. These included developing lectures on leadership with the foremost business schools and universities, and furthering my interests in researching the scientific and medical aspects of music and the brain. All these avenues opened up many new associations and honorary professorships and the commissioning of new programme projects for the BBC.

I finally departed at the end of a Beethoven cycle, and the following year Lew called me up to enquire whether I would play their last few concerts.

Each successive parting seemed blessedly gentler than the last and now it has all floated away into some distant glowing memory, still precious, but utterly unimportant.

In 2003, largely on the strength of my groundbreaking work into music and brain function and its implications for health and well-being, I was fortunate enough to be offered a three-year fellowship from NESTA (the National Endowment for Science, Technology and the Arts). In order to take up the grant I was required 'to define the source of my creativity and devise a project of work or activity that would allow me to connect more closely with it'.

Although I imagine the fellowship was given in anticipation of my further pursuit of research into musical brain function, I immediately recognised that three years spent in communion with Bach's sonatas and partitas for solo violin would take me deeply inside myself and might reveal that inner spark that was the root of any original talent I might have – and therefore my true Self. I also hoped that connecting with this essential creative source would give me the resources to live a full life following the loss of my musical family.

It was a wonderful opportunity to prepare for my final departure from the quartet, which for so long had been the mainstay of my life. It was these Bach works that came to my rescue, as they have for others at periods of loss and profound change.

Since childhood I had found myself in equal measure attracted and mystified by these strangely difficult works, and it seemed impossible to discover any single rendition that captured every aspect of the music. Over the years, every great violinist (and any number of lesser ones) have recorded these works, although quite why some of them bothered remains a mystery.

Introducing Bach's solo violin works

Bach was thirty-two years old, married and with seven children to support when he composed the six sonatas and partitas for solo violin. For this brief period he was under the patronage of Count Leopold of Anhalt-Köthen and employed as his court musician. The count was most insistent to Bach about his wanting only secular music from his brilliant employee.

Given that Bach's avowed aspiration was to create a 'complete Church music' – by which we assume he meant the composition of individual works specific to every sacred event and saint's day in the church calendar – this must have been a challenging constraint.

Such was Bach's genius and adaptability that he immediately set about composing some of his greatest and most lastingly popular works, including the Brandenburg Concertos.

Now that we consider Bach the very epitome and master of church music, we might be tempted to assume that this towering genius was a pious weakling. On the contrary, his portraits and history indicate a virile and powerful man of strong countenance and sturdy build.

Stories abound of his earlier exploits: being arrested for threatening to duel; being castigated by the authorities for taking young ladies into the organ loft; offending a town worthy by telling him his bassoon playing sounded as if he was attempting to perform an unnatural act with an unmentionable part of his own anatomy, and so on. Plainly, Bach was a thoroughly down-to-earth character.

He was also exceptionally intelligent and musically gifted, and his deep religious faith and Christian humility are always in evidence. The wealth of imaginative and vivid texts by his principal librettist Picander and others, in which the longing for spiritual union is so graphically celebrated in the symbolism of the Song of Solomon and the Psalms, suggests that Bach was a powerful and strong-minded man with an enviable libido and a healthy pride.

Although his violin sonatas were presented as purely secular works, many earlier composers, including Biber, Tartini, Corelli and others, composed similar sets of sonatas for the violin describing them as *sonate da chiesa* ('Church sonatas'), in which purely instrumental music celebrated explicitly religious agendas.

The sonatas and partitas

The sonatas and partitas by J. S. Bach are masterpieces, as beautiful and moving as they are musically complex and technically demanding. But why did Bach, the master of polyphony and counterpoint, of many-voiced music, elect to create some of his greatest and most personal work for a solo violin – an instrument that essentially plays one note at a time? To find an answer we need to look at the plethora of complex, hidden meanings that are embedded and encrypted within the music.

By great good fortune, just as I was beginning my in-depth study of these works, the German musicologist Professor Helga Thoene coincidentally released the first of her series of remarkable books revealing the hidden, esoteric codes and mysteries that have been so beautifully woven by Bach into the fabric of these extraordinary works.

Professor Thoene's dedicated research showed that Count

Leopold's insistence that Bach should compose only secular music seems to have driven the devout Bach into a secret and altogether personal dedication to God, which he achieved by constructing this music around a series of hidden chorales and other mathematical codes, all based on the central ecclesiastical calendar of Christmas, Easter and Pentecost.

The count also demanded that Bach accompany him on his extensive travels around the various fashionable 'watering holes' of Europe. In 1720 Bach returned from one such extended tour to find that his beloved wife, Maria Barbara, had died in childbirth during his absence and had already been buried.

How Bach reacted to this devastating situation is not related, but I cannot help wondering how this fine man sought to balance the purely practical issues of looking after seven motherless children while grief-stricken and yet continue to fulfil his many other professional duties.*

We do know that within days Bach was busily completing his D minor Partita, building into this apparently traditional suite of dances a complex series of mathematical and musical references that simultaneously acts as a unique musical testimonial to his dear departed wife, their children and his own profound faith in the Resurrection.

Thanks to Professor Thoene's work, these magnificent and often perplexing works are now revealed to be a devout musical tapestry drawing together creed, song, dance and mathematical coding. I believe that by expressing his faith through

* This unenviable experience has echoes of what my dear wife must have found herself facing during my illness.

these works in such an extraordinary fashion, Bach was drawing on the inspiration of previous masters as well as fulfilling his God-given mathematical genius.

The medieval church builders, artists and composers were frequently obsessed by such covert acts of worship. Many of them were greatly influenced by the tutelage of their guilds, some of which were certainly the esoteric schools of their day. These organisations often held unique knowledge and some, most obviously the Freemasons, also taught arcane systems of knowledge very like the spiritual practices that I was introduced to at the Study Society. Tradition suggests that such knowledge has been passed down by word of mouth from ancient civilisations.

This teaching was intended to encourage the initiate to follow a predetermined path, often by way of specific trials and mysteries, that could lead to a spiritual apotheosis and enlightenment. Although a certain amount is known, it is inherently difficult to establish much detail regarding these schools for they were nearly always secret, or at least very discreet, and within Lutheran circles they were also often illegal.

Another way that such esoteric knowledge has been preserved and handed down for centuries was by presenting it in eternally popular but subtly coded forms in games of skill and chance – such as chess and the Tarot. These works of Bach can also be seen to act as a public statement of hidden creeds for those with 'ears to hear and eyes to see'.

Drawing on Professor Thoene's exhaustive research, which is absolutely along the lines of my own teenage intuitions, I am convinced that in writing the sonatas and partitas Bach was practising a very personal, spiritual, algorithmic system or *schema*. There might even be a hidden reference to this in the handwritten frontispiece to the score, where he describes the works as '*Sei Solo*' ('Six Solos'), which can also be construed as meaning 'to be alone'.

When interpreted in this symbolic fashion, the numerous hidden elements within the music extend to become a great heavenly host of silent counterpoint, which fully arises in the mind of the performer and listener only to the degree that they can share and enter the composer's own secret reality.

As in life, 'meaningfulness' arises only with the perception of surrounding invisible forces. To me the irresistible attraction of such music is that its meaning can be discovered only by way of a whole myriad of psychological and symbolic interpretations.

This hidden world has everything in common with the empathic domain of my coma visions, which was similarly bizarre, coherent, moral and finally comprehensible only through deep personal reflection and analysis. Bach's solo violin works connect us directly to the mystery of life and consciousness, and the visions and dreams of NDE and coma. But they are also conduits into the special language of the personal and universal unconscious.

No other composer's music so perfectly grasps both the poetic and the mathematical inspiration that underlies our existence and need for meaning.

Crucially, in these works the limitations of the instrument oblige the listener to 'fill in' most of the polyphony, which is implied but cannot be made explicit.

The philosopher George Berkeley's writings have given rise to the question of when a tree falls in a forest without being perceived, whether there is any sound. That question is answered by this special music; these masterpieces by Bach cannot be made fully manifest without our presence. Listening is ordinarily a passive act but these works oblige us to acknowledge that a simple, attentive passivity is the best that any of us can contribute.

Thus, Bach creates a form that exquisitely conveys the miracle of 'God-made man' and, through music, justifies our human existence as meaningful.

Early on in my musical exploration, I decided that I would also need to connect myself and my performance to the dance forms that underlie so much of this music.

Like others of his era, Bach was no stranger to dance. Despite the Lutheran suspicion of all things physically enjoyable and in particular of anything erotic, Bach's world was in all probability a great deal more physical, not to say vulgar, than anything most of us now know.

The fact that this great man composed his B minor Mass while sharing one large room with his wife and many of his seventeen children gives one pause for thought. For all but a handful of princely households, life (and death) were very much experienced 'in the raw'. Courtship for the Bachs almost certainly took place while dancing, which was also the only occasion when both sexes could touch – although only briefly and while being oppressively chaperoned. Bach's mighty intellect would not have barred him from appreciating the intensity of physical 'embodiment'.

Because of this I chose to study the solo sonatas and partitas with both baroque dancers and Eurythmy – Rudolf Steiner's method of expressing language through movement.

After some years we put these elements together in performance in order to evoke the 'meaning' of the music, and in particular its many implicit threads, so that the listener could receive *all* the music as a synaesthetic (multi-sensory) integrated whole.

At the end of many years of study and performance, I found myself able to inhabit this enhanced psychological 'totality' while I performed the music. This was as close as I could conceive of 'embodying' the material world while simultaneously celebrating the moral underpinning of the abstract world.

For me this brought Bach's music very close to both the symbolic structures of my coma visions and the elevated principles of the esoteric system I had dedicated so much of my life to seeking to comprehend.

What does playing Bach feel like?

Whereas Ravel and even Janáček might be considered ravishingly skin deep and the mighty Beethoven sweeps us up into our bigger instinctive muscles, where we find ourselves locked into profoundly elemental emotions, Bach invites us into a quite different domain.

This is the place of the refined Mind. This is not to say that Bach is in any way lacking a deep compassion and profound emotional depth, but he invites us to experience this through a wonderful unification of our normally divided sense of Self.

In order to engage fully with this world view, we have to discover what it means to be at once embodied and yet detached. Perhaps 'detached' is not quite the right word; maybe 'impartial' and utterly balanced would be better.

The *Chaconne* from Partita No. 2 in D minor (BWV 1004) is the ultimate expression of this 'higher' state. It is no accident that the noble Brahms said of it that 'merely to have conceived it would have unhinged my mind', and we must remember that the many codes and other embedded meanings were totally unknown to his generation of musicians. But the best of them certainly must have sensed something uncanny in this music.

The great instrumental talents always display a marked physical poise and balance when they play. This is a mark of greatness and it is also surely indicative of an ability to recruit clear mental command matched to deep and elevated emotion, all wrapped up within a perfectly efficient and uncanny physical co-ordination. Quite a mixture! At its best such a wonderful combination of abilities allows the individual to be fully cognisant and alive to all the various elements at play in the music.

For myself, I found that when playing Ravel, Janáček and their ilk, I would commonly experience scintillating mild all-round electrical immersions and all manner of other delicious stimuli. This was as nothing when compared to the orgasmic reward of becoming possessed by Beethoven. Because I was playing with complete mindfulness, Beethoven lifted me into an elevated possibility of myself. What's more, it could do this to all of us in the quartet, rendering us a single unified organism.

But not Bach. No, this music obliged me to *lose myself* through placing everything I had at the service of the music. The result was a surprisingly consistent and reliable certainty of inner clarity. No room here for nerves or other self-indulgence. Apart from anything else there was not enough time because every aspect of myself (Mind, Body and Emotions) was fully engaged.

Quite apart from the very remarkable series of secret codes in these particular works, Bach's music is always markedly rich in different hierarchies of numerical patterns.

To take one example: in common with a number of other composers from the baroque and classical periods, many of Bach's musical phrases are straightforwardly repeated one after another. This suggests simple but pleasing patterns akin to the arching between architectural stone columns – an effect that can be heightened if the performer elects to play the first phrase more loudly and the second more quietly.

This echoing places musical shapes into a kind of familiar perceptual framework, such as our experience of the mirroring of images in water, where we might see mountain ranges inverted and repeated.

Bach does all of this as a matter of natural course, but he also shows a particular penchant for threefold phrase repetitions. Bach's manner of using this device creates a quite different set of possibilities. Often these threefold reiterations are of little arabesques with each starting on a successive step of the scale – either upwards or downwards. This means that they cumulatively create a sense of trajectory in the listener: oh, we think, so now the music is rising (or falling).

However, this is Bach, so don't rush to judgement. He will then often reverse the process, keeping exactly the same little arabesque but heading off in another direction. Fine, OK then, the two events might even have cancelled each other out. But no, this is Bach. Next he reverses the shape of the arabesque so that it is upside-down. The scale-step repetitions start again but from a different note of the scale entirely – or even in an entirely different key. This is Bach, remember. Now he's in full flight and all the mimicking and mirroring are popping up as if in some accelerating evolutionary process. The rhythms of the arabesques suddenly reverse but the directions revert to where they started and so on and so on . . .

There is no limit to such creativity. It belongs at the very heart of the human creative mind, where children play, jazz players improvise, birds sing and God rejoices.

When you are playing music of this density, believe me you need all the attention you can muster because each time you play it another set of possibilities suddenly opens up . . .

I assume this is why in his later years Carl Jung is said to have spent time each day playing in a sandbox.

It has been suggested that because Bach stood on the cusp between the medieval world and the Enlightenment, he was able to capture both the rational and the intuitive in his life and in his music, which is geometric and magical in equal measure. Bach's particular historical perspective, together with his out-standing intelligence and devotional spirituality, allowed him to use and then transcend the accepted constraint and formal control of his contemporary musical language.

In our present culture, it seems we are neurologically prone to be dominated by cognition, emotion or instinct, and the intel-lect alone is regarded as the crucible of truth. As a result, many of the finest contemporary thinkers convince themselves that emotional understanding lacks any intrinsic or objective value.

Because of this they are quite unable to grasp that most modern scientific scholarship typically inhabits only one par-ticular domain of mind and fail to recognise that without both the emotional and physical aspects of ourselves, we cannot confirm our unity with the spiritual world.

Almost devoid as it is of spiritual mystery in contemporary society, our very cleverness often stands between us and a new apperception of the Divine.

This was almost certainly not the case for Bach and perhaps only in some future millennium will a single individual once again be able to integrate the totality of current beliefs within a deep personal faith. This type of integration is the natural domain of true mysticism and true art.

Sadly this dichotomous impoverishment can also extend into our musical world.

Manoug Parikian and Bach

My first brush with Bach's works for solo violin occurred when I was about fourteen. As a special concession, Manoug invited me to choose which piece I would like to learn next and I enthused about wanting to learn some solo Bach.

He seemed surprised at this choice, although he was respectful of it, informing me that Bach's solo violin works were considered the Old Testament of the violin world while the Paganini *Caprices* represented the New Testament.

Manoug was a highly regarded and refined player with a delightful style, beautiful tone, polished technique and impeccable musical taste, but however much I revered him for all those qualities, he was no Bach player.

At a recital he gave in Oxford it was abundantly clear that he was not at all comfortable playing the great C major solo Sonata. The opening *Adagio* and the massive *Fugue* that follows it are in their own way as difficult as anything found in the repertoire, and his problems were certainly not technical

– yet I could sense that musically he was all at sea. But since he was the master and I was a mere pupil, I assiduously suppressed any such thoughts.

When I arrived the following week, struggling hopelessly with the first movement of the D minor Partita (which is one of the technically simpler movements), his own frustration and – as I now suspect – sense of bewilderment and inadequacy transformed into a rather vicious personal attack.

'Why are you making such a meal of this, Paul? You know this is really quite a simple movement.'

Flushing with embarrassment, I struggled to express my inner turmoil. 'Well, the thing is I don't really feel I can find the music. There's so much to understand in it beyond the notes that I just can't get hold of it at all. The phrasing is so elusive, it's like when I try to draw trees, I can always capture the outline of the trunk and the branches but I can never work out how to finish off each twig and leaf. I can't make the phrases end properly and the harder I try the worse it gets!'

I could see him looking at me with vexed impatience and dimly perceived that he thought one of his most promising pupils was letting him down by becoming embroiled in what to him seemed self-indulgent neurosis. Of course, he was partially right, but not entirely.

Shaking with some kind of impotent rage, which I could recognise but not comprehend, he paced agitatedly around the room.

'Well, you are certainly wasting your time with all that stuff. Because there isn't really that much in this music. It's totally straightforward. If you want to play it properly you simply play the notes, like a typist types a letter. Of course the

247

patterns are all there, but you don't need to think about them. Just play the music like an exercise and it will come out the way it's meant to. That's what these pieces are really – just exercises.'

I felt he was mindlessly reiterating a whole tradition of violin pedagogy, honourably but unthinkingly handed down from generation to generation. These platitudes instantly diminished him in my eyes from a musical giant to a pygmy.

So literal was this perception that for a moment it felt as if I were looking at him through the wrong end of a telescope, and as he shrank his voice became simultaneously distant and indistinct. I felt my own inner reality to be so much the stronger. He never fully recovered his previous status in my estimation.

We quickly moved on from Bach. Over the years I kept returning to it without success. However, I recently found one of my Bach scores, dating from when I was about fifteen, into which I had written episodes from the New Testament. Over the *Sarabande* of the D minor Partita, for example, I had written a reference to the Garden of Gethsemane and the Passion story.

These internal, imaginative connections were evoked in me some thirty or forty years before Helga Thoene's exhaustive research revealed so much more of the inner meaning and multi-layered references that lie below the surface of these compositions.

Professor Thoene's research also revealed the chorales lying hidden within these works, and she finally succeeded in deciphering a whole series of embedded alphanumeric codes.

Curiously, for a devout Lutheran such as Bach, such codes (gematria) for converting letters and words into numbers are most commonly associated with the mystical Jewish tradition of the Qabalah, although they were also known and practised for centuries by Masonic schools.

Paragrams and the Qabalah

In Bach's circle during the early 1700s there was a popular fad for mathematical, poetic devices known as 'paragrams'. Ingeniously coded numbers and letters were hidden in odes and verses, often as a subtle way of flattering patrons. As well as being intellectually stimulating for the conventional believer, such artfully applied conceits also had a touch of danger about them, for their arcane origins lay in the forbidden world of magic, alchemy and Qabalism.

If one accepts the possibility of such occult teachings influencing Bach's close circle of friends, which included such unlikely figures as the librettist Picander and a celebrated Jewish dancing master, we can imagine that such a group might well meet together to discuss philosophical and religious ideas. If so, it is hardly surprising that Bach chose to be discreet about it and left few clues for posterity.

Bach's personal Bible, which is believed to be annotated in his own hand, shows the composer painstakingly marking references in the Old Testament, particularly those referring to David playing and singing to the Lord. Bach felt a distinct affinity with the divinely inspired King David and wrote touching comments alongside the text such as 'This surely justifies the musician in the eyes of God.'

Bach's personal gematria is based on a so-called 'naive' Latin model* using the simplest of all codes: A = 1, B = 2, C = 3, and so on. In this way it is a straightforward matter to convert names into numbers. The name BACH, for example – B = 2, A = 1, C = 3, H = 8 – totals 14. The pitches B flat, A, C and B natural ('H' in German nomenclature) spell out BACH, and this musical figure occurs throughout the solo violin works at many critical and significant moments.

It could well be that Bach sought to identify himself with the inspired and truly Godly musician David, the first great biblical performer, whose name expressed as a gematria in Hebrew also gives the number 14.

Similar numerological connections are extensive. For example: J. S. Bach = 41, an inversion of 14. Joh. Seb. Bach = 70 (divisible by 14). Johann Sebastian Bach = 158 (the individual digits of which, when added together, also make 14). Bach's wife, Maria Barbara = 81.†

Other significant numbers also present themselves: Jesus Christus = 182; Sanctus = 92; Agnus Dei = 77, etc. There are many special numbers too that possess a mystical significance of their own, such as 'perfect' numbers, 'perfect square' numbers, and so on.

Esoteric numerologies of this kind can create for their practitioners an alternative reality that often acquires a deeply

---

* Almost the same as my own when as a child I successfully converted music into a series of football results!

† In this 'natural order' number alphabet I and J are both 9, and S is 18.

superstitious or magical potency. Although we can view such conversions of letters and words into 'significant' numbers as meaningless superstition, even in our supposedly rational society number magic can play a curious part. Much scientific thinking is based on the representation of observed phenomena by mathematical formulas, computer programming, statistics, economics, epidemiology and statistical medicine, etc. Our modern minds are reassured by the knowledge that apparently chaotic phenomena, such as the weather or the financial markets, possess a deeper level of order, which can be expressed in rational mathematical language as algorithms to show that apparently random events are actually but imperceptibly coherent and even ordained.

In terms of mathematical ability, Bach was a phenomenon or *savant*.[*] But unlike many celebrated contemporary *savants*, Bach was super-functioning rather than only selectively gifted.

In a sense he was also a modernist in that he applied his immense musical and mathematical gifts to the vexed issue of tempering (tuning) the scale within the limitations of his contemporary technology.

As well as composing his immense *Forty-eight Preludes and Fugues* as a proof of the usefulness of his tuning system, Bach was also the recognised authority on the construction and tuning of organs. He spent much time advising organ builders and travelling around Europe to test and perform on their newly built instruments. Nowadays, many people with gifts such as Bach's become elite computer programmers, but it was

---

[*] See Douglas Hofstadter, *Gödel, Escher, Bach*, a study into how cognition arises from apparently 'meaningless' elements within the brain.

his unique qualities that enabled him by way of music to make explicit the implicit wonders of the Universe.

The Nobel prize-winning physician, Christian philosopher and mighty organist Albert Schweitzer's famous comment, 'Above all, Bach is a mystic because all true mystics are in love with death', probably reaches as close as we can in words to the wonder of this noble mind.

Somehow when we play Bach we become locked into the Divine Mechanism of the Universe, which is the 'Mind of God'.

Schweitzer also spoke of Bach as having a 'nostalgia for death'. Whether that is true or not of Bach, it resonates with much in my own temperament.

A fascination with death

After my father was stricken with heart disease and seemed likely to die, I became fascinated by death. I took to visiting the local churchyards to draw the tombstones and I kept experiencing sudden feelings of horror, during which the earth opened up before me into some terrible underworld. These visions were remarkably prescient for they proved to be almost the same as I suffered later in life in coma.

I responded by retreating into my own internal domain together with my violin. In the meantime our family doctor advised my mother to urge me to go outside and play like other children. No wonder my poor extrovert mum found me so difficult to cope with.

This morbid and anxious phase eventually passed but its marks remained as a continuing interest in NDE and some of the more abnormal aspects of musical expression. Fortunately, all of this took on a more positive aspect when, under the influence of Dr Roles, I became inspired to research the neural correlates of musical experience within the human brain. In a nutshell perhaps, it could be said that my rest-less musical perfectionism hinged on a compulsive desire to defeat death – as I dare say much of this book is too.

My guess is that very similar motivations moved Bach to compose his solo violin works, particularly the *Chaconne*.

The Chaconne

The magnificent *Chaconne* is the final movement of the D minor Partita, and within it Professor Thoene has uncovered Qabalistic numerologies of the Creed and the Kyrie Eleison. She has also revealed bar-by-bar representations of Maria Barbara's name as well as Bach's own, and even the names of their children together with their dates of birth.

While some of the thematic chorales are hidden, almost in the manner of complex, cryptic crosswords, others form the very substance of the music itself and all carry precise refer-ences to key events in the Christian calendar. Furthermore, as one might expect from this master of polyphony, these codes are multi-levelled with some based on note names, others on note lengths and others again on pitch differences. The bar numbers and even visual notational motifs all play a part, and numbers associated with Jesus seem to have special import-ance. As ever, Bach's own 'note' signature (B flat – A – C – B natural) is also much in evidence.

The overall key structures of the sonatas and partitas are also deeply significant, with each 'church' sonata being paired with its secular partita, or dance suite.

As its mirror, the opening Sonata in G minor has a delightful Partita in B minor, which takes the form of a series of dances, each followed by a variation or 'double'. Each of these paired movements, the dance and its variation, can also be played together as a duet. However, in order to perform this doubling it is necessary to work out the mathematical ratio between them.

Quite apart from the sheer cleverness of this device, this pairing of movements fulfils another important musical function, which is that of *drama*.

Most Western music relies on at least some degree of opposition or resolution of conflict in order to give it zest. But the dance suite or formal partita form is always constructed without such modulation or different tonal nodes. How then to invest it with interest or narrative?

Part of the answer comes from the fundamental asymmetries of baroque dance itself, which actually makes much use of a device called 'oppositions'. This means that the dancer must never have one leg and its opposite arm facing in the same trajectory at the same time. In other words, while the left leg is moving forward the right arm must be going backwards.

Although this codifies an entirely natural swing of the limbs, it carries a strangely delightful and stylised manner to the dance, which is very marked when the dancers come to rest. Within the music much of this asymmetric balance is achieved by the skilful application of mirroring patterns.*

* See p. 51.

This means that at a philosophical level baroque dance and music literally 'embody' the resolutions of different polarities or contradictions. What a vast undertaking Bach's mighty *Chaconne* represents. This is a great mind seeking to resolve life and death – and, for many of us, succeeding.

The religious calendar in the sonatas and partitas

As a pair, the G minor Sonata and B minor Partita celebrate the birth of Christ and the mystery of the Incarnation in which the One becomes two. Expressed in the partita, in which each movement is followed by its variation ('double') we discover a full mystery of the singularity and duality combined.

The following pair: the A minor Sonata and the D minor Partita (which culminates in the towering *Chaconne*), celebrate the Passion, Christ's Crucifixion and the Resurrection.

The BACH motif is the underlying structural knot that holds together the wonderful 'resurrection' *Fugue* in the A minor Sonata. Although this motif runs throughout, it is explicitly stated (and even then transposed) only in the very last statement of the fugue subject, where it arrives most significantly as a *tierce de Picardie*, in which the pervasive minor key is transformed into a final triumphant major.

All the sonatas and partitas, which portray the humanity of Christ's life, are firmly fixed in the minor key, with one important exception: the mid-section of the *Chaconne*, which evokes Maria Barbara's Resurrection in Christ is a glorious chorale section in the major key.

Sadly this uniquely beautiful musical representation and celebration of Maria Barbara's relief from this 'vale of tears' is only short-lived. The *Chaconne* finishes with a depiction of Bach himself standing alone in the midst of his loss and grief. This supposedly secular composition could only be the statement of a devout believer.

The final pair are both in the major key. The C major Sonata and the triumphant E major Partita both celebrate Pentecost through the glories of a state of grace. In these two compositions, Christ has risen to sit at the right hand of God and all the movements of both works are in the major key.

The Sun King

The *Chaconne* is a seminal work, but its roots, in common with those of the other partitas, lie in the French dance suites that reached a high-water mark at the court of Louis XIV, the 'Sun King'. In his stylish and dissolute circle the members of the aristocracy dedicated themselves to perfecting their courtly manners and the skills of dance.

At this level, baroque dance was no mere pastime or simple dalliance, but assiduously studied under the tutelage of highly experienced and revered dancing masters, many of whom were Jewish, and who would often themselves play the music on little kit-fiddles as they taught.

The music for these dances developed and transformed as it rose in rank over the centuries. For example, the sarabande developed from a highly erotic and salacious dance into a much more suppressed, though still erotically tinged and melancholy, memorial dance that often featured in operas to mark the death of a main protagonist. The chaconne became attenuated into a lordly statement of temporal power and also often provided the culmination of important court operas. Louis XIV himself would customarily appear on the stage, lavishly costumed as the sun, to perform an immensely long chaconne.

The significance of this strange ritual lay in the musical form of the chaconne being founded on a fixed bass line. The form of the dance provided a perfect summation of earthly dominion by symbolising a system of planets revolving obediently around the sun, just as the courtiers were propelled in their orbits by the absolute power of the king.*

By contrast, in Bach's world, the only fixed absolute is Death and the only dominion is of Christ the Saviour. The theme he takes for the *Chaconne* is a version of Luther's hymn 'Christ lay in Death's bonds' (*Christ lag in Todesbanden*, BWV 4), while the musical narrative relates the story of Maria Barbara's blessed resurrection and the ultimate freedom made possible for all humanity in the Passion.

Post-death experience confirms this view. The external world of men and women, its activity, ambition and all the other glittering prizes, becomes visibly brittle, transient and superficial – very like the glittering figure of the Sun King himself capering all in gold above the dark realities of his court.

Though the presence of Death remains, a glimpse of Heaven is thankfully received as a saving grace and a constant place of refuge. Knowing this, the values we live by are no longer the same – how can they be?

---

* Very like my own visionary experience of revolving in space about the female aspect of the Divinity as one of a group of worshipping acolytes.

Coda

Following a musical path has given me something more than just a good life: namely a rich and meaningful one.

But I must acknowledge that my reflections do tend towards complexity.

So how best to summarise my thoughts now?

As well as teaching meditation and Ouspensky's system, the Study Society used a lovely collection of ancient Vedic myths and stories handed down from within the Advaita (or non-dualistic) teachings of northern India.

No one knows for sure the exact provenance of these time-less stories, but they each contain their own precious kernel of self-evident truth.

Across the thirty or forty years I have been familiar with them, each of these deceptively simple tales has increasingly revealed its subtle wisdom, a wisdom that, I dare say, we have barely yet begun to approach in the Western world.

When I was a child I was aware that I was not destined to share many of my parents' beliefs because mine were differ-ently shaped by my love of music.

In our Western European tradition this kind of dilemma is often explored in the many myths and stories about 'change-ling' or 'cursed' children (such as Cinderella) who are later revealed to be princes and princesses. Most of these revela-tions occur around obviously sexual 'awakenings' such as the adult stirrings of a first kiss and so on.

In the Vedic tradition this same notion is approached in a more spiritual way, as in this beautiful story of the little lion —

The Little Lion

Once upon a time an orphaned baby lion was taken in and brought up by a flock of sheep.

One day this little lion heard the terrifying roar of a full-grown lion nearby and, instead of feeling frightened like the rest of the flock, he felt a strange awakening inside him.

So powerful was this sensation that he ran off to meet up with the wild lions. As soon as they saw each other and communicated, he recognised his true nature and became a proper lion.

In my case this childhood musical awakening took the form of a cuckoo call in a song, the power of which, once I met other musicians, never left me.

When I fell in love with the violin (irrespective of whether or not this was some kind of reincarnation), this event opened up to me the spiritual salvation of the arrow maker —

The story of the arrow maker

One day an arrow maker was sitting outside his hut sharpening the tips of his arrows, when a large, rowdy and colourful wedding party passed by, all blowing trumpets, throwing flowers, singing and shouting.

After this noisy party had left a neighbour came to converse with the arrow maker.

'Well, my friend, that was quite an affair, was it not?'

The arrow maker looked up, surprised.

'Why, whatever are you referring to?'

Now his friend looked taken aback.

'Well, that great noisy crowd of wedding guests with the bridal couple, of course.'

But such was his attention to his task it was clear that his friend the arrow maker had seen and heard nothing!

Within traditional meditation teaching, the arrow maker's one-pointed attention on his arrow head describes a 'mindful' reiteration of the mantra, by which the rest of the world falls away and loses its attraction.

My attention happened to be more on the bow than the arrow and involved such things as learning to draw a straight bow stroke on the violin and the practice of scales. But these fortunately created exactly the same end point.

So while this was happening to me as I dedicated myself to my violin practice, I was quite unaware that so was a precious inner union (a *yoga* or 'marriage') between the practical, material reality of my mother's world and the idealistic and cerebral one that my father inhabited.

Then when I recognised in Heifetz's playing the possibilities of expanding instrumental attention to such an extent that it obliterated the distractions of the outside world, I was beginning to taste the elevated qualities of —

Lakshman's Dive

One day Lakshman was standing on the side of a great river (the River of Life and Death) when Arjuna passed by.

'How much I would love to see the illusion of life and death,' said Lakshman. Arjuna appealed to him not to wish for this but Lakshman insisted.

At last Arjuna took the gold ring of knowledge and wisdom from his finger and flung it into the river, saying to Lakshman, 'Oh, look, my ring – please dive in and bring it back!'

Immediately Lakshman jumped into the water, swimming into the depths to retrieve the golden ring.

As he went into the depths he forgot his previous life and his conversation with Arjuna – in fact, everything.

Instead, when he came up to the surface he saw people washing and bathing and went ashore. He met a lovely young woman, fell in love, married and had children.

At last in old age he fell in and died. As he died he once again found himself in the river, and rose to the surface, where he saw Arjuna waiting for him on the river bank.

He at once realised the truth, that all his past life had taken no time and did not register in eternity but that his conversation with Arjuna belonged to a different reality – outside time and passing events.

As well as perfectly encapsulating the expansion of focused time, this story also provides a very different model of the act of dying, in which a single moment or just a final few heartbeats of a passing life can be quite enough to experience a complete life review.

Later on, when we spent so much of our lives within the quartet trying to reconcile the Pythagorean gap, we were all gradually obliged to learn to contain the experience just as Shiva held the poison —

Shiva holds the poison

This image is so ancient that I am not sure that it is even expressed as a story. Instead it appears as a Vedic symbol or picture that shows Shiva (the God of Creation and Destruction) dancing, a dance that illustrates the dance of life itself.

However, the psychological and philosophical richness of this symbol is that while Shiva dances he is said to be holding poison in his mouth. As long as he does not swallow or spit this poison out, the Dance of Life can continue.

Playing in tune within a string quartet seems to exactly replicate this paradoxical image. The more we understood the essential impossibility of being 'right' in terms of personal tuning within an ensemble, the closer the notion of the ensemble 'dancing' only through sustained error became clear and necessary.

This principle that I have described within the conflicts of trying to play in tune as a group extends to every aspect of ensemble performance: rhythm, pulse, timbre, dynamics – everything. None of these can ever be made 'right' until every member is willing to yield their own sense of 'rightness' for the greater good.

Nowadays there is much discussion about so-called 'elephants in the room', which we generally understand to mean some problem so massive or awkward that people will do anything they can to avoid acknowledging it.

But the original Sanskrit elephant had far more psychological subtlety and probably dates back some thousands of years —

The Elephant in the village of the blind

Once upon a time a mighty elephant was taken by his mahout into a small village in which all the inhabitants were blind.

All the villagers were naturally terribly excited to find out what this fabulous animal was like and so they moved cautiously forward, hands outstretched, hoping to find out.

As each person reached the elephant they each began to describe what they had found.

The one whose hand landed on the elephant's tail insisted that the creature was like a strong stick. His neighbour, who was feeling the immense tusks, described an animal that was hard as rock. Another man, who was stroking the trunk, began disputing with both his colleagues, telling them that, on the contrary, the elephant was unusually yielding and flexible . . . and so it went on.*

Even though the 'blindness' of our situation is psychologically self-imposed, as long as we insist on 'our' vision being the only valid one, it must be impossible for any one person to comprehend the totality.

How then can we change this?

Dedication to the work of the group certainly, but at the same time there are other paths to be pursued.

---

* This was always our predicament when approaching some fine score new to us. As I have attempted to describe, each Beethoven movement started life with every one of us insisting upon the 'truth' of our personal partial vision: 'No it's a bendy trunk; no, a set of massive feet; of course not, looky here, it's two great sharp ivory tusks and so on . . .'

As I have intimated throughout this book, I have come to the conclusion that our ultimate dilemma is how to define and discover Ourselves.

Through Self-reflection, of course. By discovering ourselves within others, which is merely a different kind of reflection; yes, naturally. By a contemplation of the Infinite; yes, by all means.

Because finally all of these are one and the same, looking inwards or casting our eyes outwards towards the Infinite ultimately reveal the same Self.

So Bach's six solo sonatas and partitas marked 'Be Alone' reflect the sacred truth, that the best we can aspire to is, as Jung has it, to meet Ourselves coming the other way.

Which is very like the enlightened Sanskrit concepts of Turiya and Samadhi, in which 'I am all this' and 'All this, I am.'

Appropriately enough, this sacred culmination of Self-enlightenment is recounted through the story of the two artists – a lovely story about the nature of truth and divinity, and how we reflect each other's being —

The two artists

There were once two artists who visited a king, offering to decorate his throne room. Their proposal was an intriguing one since they promised to make two identical pictures, one at each end of the hall.

Furthermore, they undertook to do this without being able to see each other.

Intrigued, the king accepted their commission and in order

to ensure that they stuck to their promise, he ordered a screen to be constructed, dividing the room.

After many arduous weeks of work the artists finally announced that their task was complete.

On the appointed day the king and his courtiers crowded into the throne room, where he ordered the screen to be removed.

At one end one of the artists (the *Manas*) had painted a rich and exquisite representation of the world, while at the other end the other artist (the *Bhuddi*) had spent his time polishing the wall so perfectly that it reflected every mark on the opposite wall.

As well as telling us much about the nature of truth and the aspiration of our psyche, this story has much to tell us about love and how and why we might discover how to love and work with others.

As in all such stories, the Self is not represented by the protagonists, who are merely symbols of the agency of the mind, but by the king (the *Atman*) whose role it is to be the silent observer relishing the play.

One of the most ancient Sanskrit Hindu symbols is two small birds, which are said to be an illustration of our fundamental human consciousness. This symbol is about as deceptively simple as hearing the two notes of a cuckoo's call —

The two birds

There are two birds in a tree.

One bird flits from branch to branch singing, while the other simply sits silently watching and listening.

What a wonderful summation of musical performance, including all the recursive possibilities we can bring to it.

When all the tragedy and drama are finished, the bombs have stopped dropping, Wotan has dissolved Valhalla and life is over, what are we left with?

Two sounds continue to resonate in the still air and infinite silence: birdsong and children's laughter.

If we are still there to hear them, we might think they are angels singing, and we would be right.

Our time on earth is brief but my own hope is to be able to leave this world with the lightness of a small bird – and if I am given the grace to hear a cuckoo as I depart I shall consider myself truly blessed.

After all:

> You are the music, while the music lasts.
>
> T. S. Eliot

The Medici Quartet ———————————

1968   Paul Robertson wins a scholarship to the Royal
        Academy of Music, London
1971   The Medici Quartet is formed at the Royal Academy
        of Music

> Paul Robertson *violin*
> David Matthews *violin*
> Paul Silverthorne *viola*
> Anthony Lewis *cello*

1973   The quartet makes its debut at the Wigmore Hall,
        London
        Awarded three-year residency at York University
1975   Recording contract with EMI Records
        Teaching residency at Kingston University, Surrey
        The Quartet starts playing with pianist Clifford
        Curzon
1976   Performance series with the Royal Shakespeare
        Company based on composers' lives, directed by
        John Caird and Cordelia Monsey
1979–96 Visiting residency at the University of Lancaster
1982   Ivo-Jan van der Werff joins the quartet as violist

1988–90	Complete Beethoven quartet cycle for Nimbus Records
1991	Colin Callow joins the quartet as second violinist
1993	Cathy Thompson joins the quartet as second violinist
1996	Television series, *Music and the Mind*, written and presented by Paul Robertson
	The quartet is appointed artists-in-residence at the University of Surrey
	Steve Morris joins the quartet as second violinist
2000	Cathy Thompson rejoins the quartet as second violinist
2007	Paul Robertson leaves quartet after a final Beethoven cycle at the Petworth Festival
2008	Paul Robertson returns to lead and organise the quartet's 'farewell' concert tour which is curtailed by Paul's medical emergency
2009	The quartet reconvenes to play Tavener's *Towards Silence*
2013	The first performance of Tavener's *Scatter Roses Over My Tears*
2016	Wigmore Hall lecture–recital *Cavatina: The Inner Life of Ensemble*, Paul Robertson in conversation with Tia Kuchmy, reuniting past and present members of the quartet

Acknowledgements —————————————————

This was never intended to be a long book and fortunately, now isn't. Along the lines of the oft ascribed apology that '*I have made this longer than usual because I have not had time to make it shorter*', the relative brevity of this book thankfully exists at the price of innumerable kind, generous and supportive friends, family and other colleagues who have paid the undoubtedly turgid sacrifice of thrashing through its many interminable previous incarnations. To these numerous skillful and generous-hearted optimists, I can only offer my heart-felt thanks.

Along the way, as I now realise, close family members were obliged to take up the role of professional musical intimates, whilst my Quartet colleagues found themselves continually embarrassed to inhabit the role of close siblings. Nor did I hesitate to inflict equivalent compromises upon my many other unfortunate friends, who became similarly encumbered with the unforgiving task of trying to prune a jungle, and yet continued to behave with their typically characteristic compassion and concerned commitment.

An unexpected but entirely welcome six-month fellowship in 2014 to the Wissenschaftskolleg, Berlin offered me a wonderful opportunity to finish the larger part of the writing, after which my dear good friend Gerald Beckwith heroically stepped in to take on this impossible task, which he did with commendable clear-sightedness and intelligence, despite his own personal circumstances which would have overwhelmed most normal people at the time. I must also express my sincere gratitude to my dear friends Hugh Pidgeon and Tony Pinching for their tireless work as well.

I am wholly mindful of my great good fortune in having finally been taken under the skilled and loving care of Patrick, Annabel, and Belinda, Jill and Kate as part of the formidable team at Faber's.

Picture credits

All photos courtesy of the author except: *Professor Richard Guyatt* © Anthony Blake; *Sir Clifford Curzon* © Fritz Curzon; *Medici Quartet 1982*, photo by Johan Fjellstrom; *Music and the Mind* Channel 4 Television, photo by Margaret Williams.